MIRACLE
The Long Journey Home

Maureen Kincaid

ISBN 978-1-0980-8384-7 (paperback)
ISBN 978-1-0980-8385-4 (digital)

Christian Faith Publishing, Inc.
832 Park Avenue
Meadville, PA 16335
www.christianfaithpublishing.com

Printed in the United States of America

DEDICATION

To Laura, whose life on earth ended much too early
But whose spirit has impacted my life
more than anyone I've known.

And to my parents, Ann and Thomas Kincaid,
Who loved me unconditionally even when I
was miserable and at my worst and
who laid the foundation for my Catholic faith.

PREFACE

Writing this book has been on my bucket list for many years; however, had I written it twenty, ten, or even one year ago, it would have been a very different story. My original conception of the book was to share my story of survival—survival of a horrific event that occurred on November 29, 1979, which resulted in the death of my friend, Laura, and forty years of trauma for me and the others that were present that night. Some aspects of my survival story as a result of this trauma are shared; however, the main focus is on my forty-year journey of forgiveness and the way God has shepherded me. His shepherding led me not only to meet the man who murdered my friend and caused tremendous pain and trauma in my life but also to develop a deep spiritual friendship with him.

It is my hope that this story will help others who have experienced violent crimes to heal and learn the importance of, and in fact, the *necessity* of engaging in forgiveness if one is going to fully regain control of their destiny and experience full healing. The title reflects several aspects of my forty-year journey. I selected the main title, *Miracle*, for two reasons. First, I believe that God has truly performed a miracle in my life and the life of the perpetrator of the crime that occurred forty years ago. To go from complete hatred of an individual to deep love and respect for that individual is a true miracle in the making. Secondly, miracle is the nickname that I have been given by the man who committed the murder of my friend.

The subtitle "The Long Journey Home" also has multiple meanings for me. As a cradle Catholic, I went through the motions of going to mass but saw little to no value in using my Catholic faith to guide my life. I merely went to mass to fulfill the "holy obligation." However, forty years later, I look to God for everything in my life. I have taken a forty-year journey back to the arms of my Loving Father, whom I rejected immediately following that tragic night. Because of the span of my faith journey, the process of full healing was also quite long. Yet, it never would have occurred had I not come full circle to meet the man who murdered my friend, establishing a lifelong relationship with him.

It has truly been a long journey home and an absolute miracle in my life, one that I hope will help many victims of violent crimes and/or anyone who needs to forgive so that they can fully heal their heart and mind.

ACKNOWLEDGEMENTS

First and foremost, I thank our heavenly Father for His endless love, mercy, grace, blessings, and for the incredible miracle that He manifested in my life. I am forever grateful for His sacrifice so that we can all be forgiven for our sins and live with Him in everlasting life.

I am truly grateful for my partner of twenty-five years, Maureen Scott, for her love and support throughout my forgiveness journey and for her commitment to growing together in faith.

I thank my family and friends for their love, continual encouragement, and support in my journey of forgiveness. A special thanks to Nancy, Mary Beth, Kris, Kathleen, Erica, and Crystal for reviewing my manuscript and providing feedback and editing assistance.

I am also thankful for the love and support of my brothers and sisters from Our Lady of Mercy parish especially those from my CRHP and Alpha teams. I am grateful for my Alpha and CRHP-sister, Sharon who accompanied me on one of the prison visits and who has supported and encouraged me throughout my journey.

I am grateful to my childhood friend, Marcia, who allowed me to work for her on the night of November 29, 1979. I literally begged her to let me work for her and after some reluctance, she agreed. I know it was God's plan for me to be there and Marcia was part of that plan and allowed it to happen. I pray that the guilt Marcia has carried throughout these years is completely washed away when she reads my story and can see how working that night was part of my destiny.

Finally, I thank Peter for fully devoting his life to our heavenly Father and His Son Jesus Christ in 1997 so that God's miracle could be manifested in both of our lives. I am truly grateful for his loving friendship and spiritual mentoring.

CHAPTER 1

November 29, 1979

In 1979, I was living a pretty idyllic life in Oak Forest, Illinois, a south suburb of Chicago. My family had moved there from the southside of Chicago during the "white flight" out of the city that occurred in the late 1960s. Many of the families relocated to Oak Forest from our southside neighborhood of Roseland, as well as other neighborhoods in Chicago because of the racial tensions that were occurring in the city. This migration of Caucasian families to the suburbs resulted in a community with no racial diversity and strong racist undercurrents.

I was the youngest of four children, two boys and two girls. We were a typical middle-class family, raised by hardworking parents who provided a modest lifestyle for our family. I was a good student and was involved in athletics throughout my childhood and into high school. Early in my high school years, I determined that my goal was to become a teacher, and I was set to attend a university nearby starting in the fall of 1980, as the first in my family to attend college. Although I lived a rather ordinary middle-class life, I felt fortunate for the way my parents had raised me and the life they provided. Life was good!

On the night of November 29, 1979, all that changed. I went to work at McDonald's, a job I had for two years. I was not scheduled to work that night, but my friend Marcia asked if I would work for her so she could travel down state to see our high school's volleyball team play in the state tournament. Little did I know that saying yes to her request would dramatically alter the course of my life and the lives of all those present in McDonald's that night.

I was excited to work that night because I was working with two of my favorite people. One was the manager, a kind, hardworking twenty-two-year-old woman whom I admired and looked up to. The other was my friend, Laura, who was a very funny and joy-filled person. She frequently played pranks on people and was always very upbeat and happy. Laura had us laughing several times throughout that night with her quick wit and showing us her dance moves. We all talked about how excited we were to be going down state the next morning to cheer on our team. Laura was not only a funny person, but one of the kindest and most supportive people I knew at that time. If I were down, she would always say something encouraging to lift me up. For a sixteen-year old, she was wise beyond her years. I loved taking breaks with her when we were scheduled to work on the same day and talking with her briefly every day during certain passing periods at school. Laura's joyful spirit really showed when she was out on the football field doing routines with the Pompon squad. She was president of the junior class and an exceptional student and human being. On the night of November 29, the life of this beautiful young woman, with so much promise, would come to a screeching halt, and her family and friends would never again experience the joyfulness that she brought to our lives.

Shortly after we closed that night, I was getting ready to take out the grease trap, and I asked one of my coworkers to open the back door for me. Suddenly, I felt someone grab the top of my arm with great force from behind, and I felt something pushed into my side. As I turned, I saw a black man and a gun. My immediate thought was this has to be a joke, but I quickly realized it was not. After he pulled me over to the manager's desk, he proceeded to pull each of the other employees to that central location. One of the girls had gone downstairs, and he must have been in the store long enough to know this because after he pulled me to the desk, he quickly went around the corner to get her as she came back up the stairs. When he was briefly out of sight, the manager was able to push the silent alarm. I will never forget the terrified look on Carol's face as he brought her around the corner with the gun held to her head as she whimpered.

The whole time he was gathering us to the central location, the manager was telling him she knew why he was there, and she would get him the money but asked that he please not hurt anyone. Laura and another girl were the last people he moved to the manager's desk, and as soon as he approached the desk with the two of them in front of him, I heard a pop, and Laura fell to the ground, hitting the desk as she went down. It was all so surreal and was as if I was watching something in slow motion. The manager then told all of us to get down, and we briefly knelt on the floor. None of us truly understood at that point the gravity of what had happened. I remember thinking that maybe Laura fainted. The pop sounded like a firecracker rather than a gunshot, although I had never heard a handgun fired other than on TV or in the movies. It all felt so unreal. Then he forced all but two of us into the refrigerator, leaving the manager by the safe and Laura lying on the floor.

Holding a gun to the head of the manager, he demanded she open the safe, while counting from one to ten out loud. The safe combination had recently been changed because of a change in ownership, so it took the manager what seemed like an eternity to open the safe. She struggled to remember the combination and had to go to her wallet to get the piece of paper on which the combination was written. As we watched from the refrigerator, it was terrifying to see him hold the gun to her head, counting as she struggled to open the safe. What if she could not get it open? Was he going to shoot her? Was he going to shoot us all?

By this time, the phone was ringing, and the police were outside banging on the back door in response to the silent alarm. Once the manager was finally able to get the safe open, he put her in the refrigerator with the rest of us and closed the door. The manager quickly stacked crates and boxes in front of us, as a barricade, in case he returned and started shooting. I will never forget the feeling of guilt and sadness I had at the fact that we had to leave Laura out there alone. Hovering behind the crates and clinging to one another, we waited in the refrigerator for what seemed like an eternity, not knowing who would open that door. When the door finally did open, we were faced with several guns pointing at us, but praise be to God, they were guns held by police officers. As they led us out of the refrigerator and quickly out the back door, I could not help but notice that Laura remained on the floor in that same spot. We would later learn that she died instantly from a gunshot wound to the back of her head.

There were a lot of police cars outside—more than I had ever seen before. A female police officer comforted us, letting us know we were safe, as she drove us to the police station. Once at the station, we called our parents to tell them what happened, and I remember feeling very dazed and confused, and I even told my mom that she did not have to come to the police station and that I would get a ride home from someone. The officers took us to a room and gave us some water, and we sat there waiting for an update about Laura. The whole time I sat there waiting, I was planning how I would visit Laura in the hospital the next day. Then Becky's mom came in and said, "There's no other way to tell you girls this, but Laura died."

Once we heard the news of Laura's death, we were all devastated. One would think that we would have been prepared for this, but unless you have been through trauma, it is difficult to understand how surreal it is. We all started screaming and then crying, thinking it could not be true. She can't be gone. She was only sixteen years old and had her whole life ahead of her. I became hysterical and felt like I was going to be sick to my stomach. As I began hyperventilating, I was taken to another room, where paramedics attended to me and put an oxygen mask on me. I had a weird sensation in my feet and hands, like someone was sticking needles in them. They made us stay at the station for a while, but eventually, they put me on a stretcher and took me to the hospital, along with two of the other girls.

While in the emergency room, I was given a sedative to help me calm down. Then Monsignor O'Day, one of our parish priests came to see me. Perhaps as a result of the sedative, or the trauma of fearing for my life, or the shock of a dear friend shot and killed by an armed robber, I could not quite make sense of what was happening. I wrote of Father O'Day's visit in my journal: "that was the weirdest feeling—I felt like I was on my deathbed, and he was there to give me my last rites." A part of me wished I were dying because it would be so much easier than dealing with the extreme pain, grief, and terror that was plaguing me at the time.

We also learned that the police had caught the man who committed the armed robbery and murder, as he shot out a window in the front of the McDonald's, crawled out, and ran down the main road with the police chasing him. He eventually crawled into a Good Will box near the local Jewel Food Store and was apprehended by the police. After a high-speed chase, the police also apprehended the accomplices waiting out in the getaway car, who left the scene once they heard sirens.

When I got home around 3:30 a.m., I sat in the kitchen for a while, not really comprehending what had just happened and eventually went to bed. As I woke up the next morning at eight, I remember lying in my bed, staring at the ceiling in a daze and hoping it was all a nightmare, but of course, it was not. I don't think I said two words to my parents, and they said very little to me. What was there to say? I was completely numb and felt like I was walking in a fog. I am certain that my parents were going through their own trauma, knowing that they could have lost *their* daughter that night—they could be planning my funeral. This would eventually cause a short-term strain in my relationship with them, particularly with my mom because I could not understand why she did not want to talk about it when that was all I thought about. It truly became an obsession—all I thought about and all I wanted to talk about, reliving that night over and over and over. It was almost as if I was punishing myself for surviving.

The trauma of waking up the next day to discover it was not a nightmare was compounded by the fact that I needed to go the state's attorney's office to answer questions and to identify the gunman in a lineup. The thought of facing him again, even if there was a wall/window between us, was truly horrifying, and I was terrified that I would not be able to identify him. What if I could not pick him out in the lineup—would they let him go? Facing a line of several African American men, I knew right away which one was him, but the tension of it all was unbearable. The questioning was also very stressful because they put a lot of pressure on us to remember everything. If one of us remembered something like the doorbell ringing or a second gunshot but others didn't, they badgered, asking, "Why are you the only one that remembers this?" In retrospect, I am certain they were just trying to document all the details of the night in preparation for criminal charges.

The days following were a blur, culminating with attending the two-day visitation and the funeral of my friend, who died so senselessly at the age of sixteen. This event truly rocked our community and our school. We had never experienced this level of violence and criminal activity. Our high school was tremendously affected due to Laura's popularity with not only other students, but with the faculty and staff. Unlike today, when schools bring in counselors following a traumatic event, there was no support available for us. There was only one teacher in my entire high school, my honors algebra teacher, Barb Marstellar, who approached me and let me know that she was there if I needed to talk. I regularly went to her classroom after school. I did not always talk about what happened that night, but it just felt good to know someone was concerned about me. It seemed like everyone else, just like my parents, did not want to talk about it. If we don't talk about it, it will go away. This was very painful for me, as I was just desperate for help to deal with my pain and trauma. I now know that the teachers and staff were all also grieving and probably just did not know how to help us. We needed to talk and to process the tremendous loss and trauma we experienced. We needed someone to listen. We needed so much more than what was provided.

Returning to work at McDonald's was extremely difficult. Being back in that environment obviously triggered memories of that night. My senses were particularly heightened—walking by the desk where he gathered us and where Laura lost her life, walking into that refrigerator, where we all hid behind stacks of food and drink, wondering if he was coming back for us, even just looking at the red tile on the floor where her body lay so still. It was all so overwhelming. I do not know why I returned to work, but I left after a few weeks because of the painful memories I experienced and the way I was treated by management. I had requested to not work the closing shift again unless there was an armed guard on duty. The managers granted my request, but on my next performance evaluation, I was rated lower in several areas of performance. Given the fact that I had always had very strong evaluations, I knew that there was something very wrong, and I quit. It could have been related to the fact that two of us and Laura's family had filed a civil lawsuit against McDonald's for several reasons, one of which was a defective back door that was never repaired, even though management received notice that the door did not consistently latch when it was closed. It is the door through which the gunman entered. Or it could have simply been related to the fact that I refused to work the closing shift without an armed security officer on duty. Regardless of the reason for the poor treatment, it was critical that I not return to an environment that repeatedly put me through the torture of reliving the events of that horrific night, especially with no support.

November 29, 1979, was truly the worst night of my life. What I would come to learn decades later, November 29, 1979, was also the most influential night of my life, helping me to find my way back to God.

CHAPTER 2

———— ❦ ————

The Gunman

He was born March 30, 1960, in Chicago, Illinois, one of three children born of a mother who was a "preacher's kid" and a second-generation Chicago native. His father had a third-grade education and migrated to Chicago in the early 1950s from Mississippi as part of the last wave of African Americans who left the South and settled in Chicago during the early twentieth century looking for a better life. When his parents met, his mother had two children, Crystal and Carlene. When his mother and sisters moved from Chicago's westside to the southside to live with his dad, there were two renters occupying the two bedrooms of that apartment, leaving Crystal and Carlene to sleep on a "let-out-couch" in the dining room. His mother would quickly change that and insisted that the renters move.

With a new baby boy on the way, and in order to make up for the loss of income from the renters, they needed to find a way to supplement their income, so his father accepted an offer from another Mississippian to receive money for hosting illegal poker games in the apartment once a month on weekends. These games included hustlers, drug dealers, robbers, and convicted felons, some of whom had committed murders. His mother made sure that the children were not home when these games occurred. She wanted the best for her children and dreamed that they would all attend college.

When he was six years old, his mother became a school-crossing guard so she could spend more time with her three children. She and his father were proud of their precocious son, who developed into a kind, compassionate, and caring little boy and eventually young man. He was a jokester and very witty but also very active in church and enjoyed engaging in fellowship with other children. His younger cousins looked up to him because of these positive character traits. His sister Crystal remembers his dancing, looking and acting like Michael Jackson. She also remembers about how compassionate he was as a young adolescent, comforting her after the early death of her husband. He came to stay with her one summer when she was a teacher in an upward-bound program and assisted her and the other staff with the activities. Although he was younger than the high school teens in the program, no one ever knew it. Because of his personality and maturity, the upward-bound youth looked up to him, and the staff and administrators of the program were impressed with his leadership.

His parents separated when he was eight years old for many reasons, one of which was his mother's desire to discontinue hosting weekend poker games. His father begged to keep his son with him. Although his mother allowed him to live with his father, she spent time with her son every day after school. His father continued to host poker games, but now, instead of once a month, they took place every weekend. Thus, the influence of people who gambled, used drugs, and engaged in criminal activity continued. He heard frequent stories of criminal activity, during which these older men boasted about drug deals, burglaries, and other crimes. As a boy, he was gullible, impressionable, and fascinated with the "fast money" about which these criminals bragged. He was introduced to drugs by these people, whom he had grown to admire and respect, and he joined in because he did not want them to think he was "square." By the age of fifteen, he regularly used marijuana and cocaine.

Despite his mother's attempt to keep watch over and protect him, it was the criminal friends of his parents that had the greater influence on him. Like his father, he was enamored with the wads of cash, jewelry, fancy clothes, and fine cars that these people owned, as compared to his parents' minimal possessions. His mother was unaware of this influence, as he continued to attend church with her every Sunday and maintained his cheerful and charming personality around her.

Although he moved back in with his mother when he entered high school, he continued to get drugs from some of the poker players, as well as from his Uncle Edward. It was not uncommon for him to smoke marijuana and snort cocaine on a daily basis. Even though he attended church every Sunday with his mother, he coveted the lifestyles of the drug dealers and gamblers, some of whom still visited his house. His mother was completely unaware of the influence these men and Uncle Edward had on him. Ironically, one of his other uncles, Frank, was a minister and ended up being among his greatest supporters once he was incarcerated. Unfortunately, as an impressionable teenager, he chose the wrong uncle to respect and aspire to emulate.

Both his sisters, considerably older, attended college and seemed to escape the influence of the drug dealers and gamblers who visited their house. Despite his high IQ, he was frequently told by his white teachers that he was not "college material," so he didn't aspire to follow in his sisters' footsteps; he thought it wasn't possible. In spite of his regular use of drugs and alcohol, friends and family members considered him a "goodie two shoes" because of the strict upbringing and curfew that his mother enforced during his early preteen and teen years. But he had a secret desire to be a rebel, and Uncle Edward was willing to help him and some of his cousins become the black sheep of the family, just like Uncle Edward had become in his family. They all kept each other's secret until his mother started noticing that the happy-go-lucky son she raised, was in a stupor on many days. In the summer of 1976, his mother admitted him to a psychiatric ward in a Chicago hospital, and he was evaluated daily by psychologists and released two weeks later. After his release, his cheerful and happy demeanor returned. He finished high school and was attending a community college in Chicago in 1979.

His father died that year, which was devastating to him, and his drug and alcohol use once again increased. In July 1979, while driving his mother's rental car, two friends talked him into driving them to a McDonald's in a nearby suburb. He was high and drunk. When they arrived at the McDonald's, his friends told him to drive to the back of the building where they accosted an employee and held him at gunpoint with a starter pistol and forced the young man into their car. As the driver, he panicked and began driving away, not knowing where he was going, while his friends were screaming at him. They were caught, and he was charged with accessory to armed robbery, kidnapping, and unlawful restraint and was eventually released on bail. From that day forward, his life began to spiral out of control.

On November 15, 1979, the condo he and his mother lived in caught fire, and they lost most of their personal property because they did not have fire insurance. Although his older sister, Crystal, owned the condo and promised their mother that she would pay for her to stay in a hotel, his mother decided to remain in the condo until the repairs could be made. He, however, still trying to hide his intensified drug use from his mother, decided to use the fire as an excuse to leave the condo and move in with his Uncle Edward's family. They lived next door to his girlfriend, Michelle. Michelle was three months pregnant with his child at this time, and he stopped attending college so that he could get a full-time job to support her and their unborn child. She frequently talked about the need to get money and told him that she could steal her aunt's gun for him to use to scare someone into giving him money.

On the morning of November 29, 1979, his mother drove him to court for a continuance on the kidnapping and armed robbery charges incurred that July. He was hung over from the drugs and alcohol he consumed the night before. After the court hearing, he went back to Michelle's house and continued drinking and doing drugs. His mother's extreme disappointment in him, the fire and destruction of their condo and personal belongings, and Michelle's pregnancy all sent him into a state of distress and depression. He had reached the point of sheer desperation, needing money, not only to support his unborn child, but to help with his mother's condominium, as he felt guilty that Crystal was making the mortgage payments. Knowing that the only reason they got caught in the previous armed robbery was because he was an inexperienced "get away" driver, he and Michelle began developing a plan for how they could more effectively commit an armed robbery.

While at Michelle's house on November 29, 1979, a friend, Andre, stopped by, and the plan began to unfold. Michelle would steal her aunt's handgun, and Andre would be the driver. They would drive to the suburbs, rob a McDonald's, and run with the money. In order to get up the courage to commit this crime, he consumed large amounts of wine, marijuana, and cocaine throughout the day and evening. Crystal called him that night, after hearing from their mother that she was afraid that "the streets had gotten a hold of him." She could tell from his sarcastic tone and his raised voice that something was not right. This was the first time he had ever raised his voice with Crystal. She expressed her concern and urged him to stop whatever he was doing that was causing him to behave in a way that was shocking to her. Unfortunately, he abruptly cut her off and said he had to go because Michelle was there. Then they drove to the McDonald's in Oak Forest, Illinois. When they arrived, they noticed the back door was cracked open. Michelle gave him the gun, and he entered through the back door, and the terror of the night began.

CHAPTER 3

—— ⟨✧⟩ ——

Reliving and Managing the Trauma

The years following the robbery and murder were extremely difficult. I had gone away to college, which was another life-changing event. I knew no one, except for my roommate who was one of my best friends in high school. However, shortly before we left for college, she met a man and began a serious relationship. Because of this, she went home every weekend and sometimes even during the week and eventually transferred to a university closer to her home. With time, I met some nice people on my dorm floor and established some friendships. Albeit, these were not close friendships; thus, I did not feel comfortable sharing the traumatic event that I experienced or the continued grief and anxiety that I was still experiencing. I also continued to suffer from extreme guilt—why was I not the one that was shot and killed that night? Why was Laura the chosen one? "Survivor's guilt" is real, and it is extremely painful and tormenting. But who wants to hear about sadness and pain? No one; so I went through my college years, only talking about the terrors of the night with one of the other women who also worked at McDonald's that night, and even that was hard. I did not even talk about it with my family members. In fact, most of my family members will learn of the trauma I experienced for the first time when they read this book.

The friendships I had in college were very superficial, and my old friendships with high school friends fizzled, mostly because I pushed people away. I thought they didn't understand what I was going through. Of course, they didn't understand. How could they? In my journal, six months after Laura's murder, I wrote: "I have grown farther apart from some of my friends because of what happened. Everyone wants me to get better and be happy again, so they try saying things like 'you have to go on living' or 'Laura wouldn't want it this way.' Things like this just turn me off. Even if they do mean to help." I wanted to be happy and enjoy life, but every time I found myself doing this, I started to feel guilty. How could I have fun when Laura was no longer able to?

For over a year, I was plagued with ongoing nightmares and was afraid to be out at night alone. My fear was overwhelming and tormenting, causing me to constantly be looking behind me when out at night. I even thought that maybe he would send someone to kill me too. It was truly paralyzing at times. In a journal entry written at eight months, I wrote: "I've had a lot of nightmares about this. I dream that it happens again and again, but not always the same place. Sometimes, I get shot and there is always a gun." The Fourth of July was also a very challenging time, given the similarity of the sound of the gun and the sound a firecracker makes. In my journal entry of July 1980, I wrote, "The Fourth of July was terrible for me. Every time a firecracker went off, I jumped. Anytime I hear a popping or banging noise, I jump." Additionally, I regularly had periods of emotional hysteria and panic attacks, feeling as though I would never get through the painful time.

I also had irrational thoughts about death for quite some time after that night. In my journal entry of September 1980, I wrote, "It is 11:50, and a weird thought just entered my mind. I had a feeling that the tower (my dorm) was going to start on fire. I don't know why. I was just reading my psychology book and thought of it. Yesterday when I was riding to a state park, I suddenly had a thought that my mom was getting in a car accident. Anyone could die at any time. It scares me so much. Right now, someone I know could be dying." I visited the cemetery regularly, hoping to get some comfort from that, but it only caused me to further question my faith. In my journal entry of September 1980, I wrote, "I don't know why, but if I don't go (to the cemetery) for a while I always want to go. I don't know why, but it makes me feel better if I go. I don't know if it makes me feel like I've spent special time with her—which is crazy because she's not really there. But where is she then? Heaven? Is there such a place? I'm in a state of confusion about the whole thing?" I was really struggling with who God was and why He would allow this vibrant, joyful young woman to be ripped from her family and from our world so senselessly. How can I believe in a God that allows this to happen?

A very troubling effect of the trauma was that I became racist and afraid of people who were African American. As I read through my journal forty years later, I was horrified and ashamed at the frequent use of the N word. I also wrote about being afraid of people who were African American, especially at night. I made sweeping generalizations—because an African American man terrorized us and murdered my friend, all African Americans became bad and scary people in my mind. I had taken on the racist beliefs of the community in which I was raised.

In 1981, the sentencing of the gunman finally took place. There was no trial because he pled guilty to first-degree murder in order to avoid the death penalty. Coming face-to-face with him in the courtroom was overwhelmingly difficult, and I was once again flooded with memories of that night. Seeing him act like he was mentally unstable angered me. Although the death penalty was an option, I did not want him to get that sentence. I wanted him to live a long time in prison so he could think about how he took Laura's life and traumatized all of us that night. I wanted him to suffer and be tortured with thoughts of what put him there. I had a deep rage and hatred toward him. Life in prison would make him think about it every day for the rest of his life. And that is exactly what he received—a life sentence with no possibility of parole. Justice was done.

After the sentencing and graduating college, I stumbled through life trying to be happy, but that horrible part of my life was always hanging over my head. It was as if I was living two lives. I lived my "regular" life as a teacher, where I had to put on a happy face to hide the extreme pain that was buried deep. Then I had this secret part of my life that very few people knew about, so I was left to deal with it on my own most of the time. I regularly tried to drown my sorrows in alcohol and even dabbled in drugs for a short period of time. Drinking and doing drugs helped me to momentarily escape and forget about the deep pain and sorrow I was experiencing; however, none of that made it better. In fact, it almost always made it worse.

After many years of delay, the civil trial against McDonald's finally occurred in March 1989. Unlike the sentencing, the civil trial was a grueling experience. Testifying about that night dredged up all the memories again, and even worse, the lawyers for McDonald's implied that those of us that were present that night were to blame for what happened. They suggested that we surely did something wrong to allow the gunman in, and we just were not being honest about what took place that night. Reliving the tragic night was bad enough, but being blamed for what happened was unbearable. The trial lasted over a week, and the jury's verdict ruled in favor of us, the victims. Justice was done. Although this would not bring Laura back, it is my understanding that as a result of our civil case, security measures at all McDonald's restaurants were improved—making the additional suffering and stress all worthwhile.

In addition to the two court experiences, there were daily triggers. For over a decade, with the exception of the short time I returned to work, I did not enter a McDonald's restaurant. The red-tiled floor was a huge trigger for me—the floor where she lay. Going into restaurants in general, especially at night, was extremely difficult. Regardless of the time of day, I needed to (and still do) sit in a position where my back is not facing the door because the gunman had come from behind. Elevators and other closed spaces were and continue to be difficult for me, especially for any length of time because of the time we spent in the refrigerator. For years, I had dreams about being stuck in an elevator, and then the elevator would plummet at a high rate of speed. While I was filled with fear in circumstances where these triggers occurred in the early years, with time I learned to manage my fear and anxiety in these situations, limiting the stress.

Two of the most difficult triggers for me are related to the intrusion and the "mess" that occurred during that night, as well as the uncertainty of waiting for the terror to end as we were in the refrigerator. After Laura had been shot, and in the process of us all getting down on the ground, the grease trap that I had been carrying and set down when the gunman took me to the desk tipped and seeped over the floor and by Laura's body. Additionally, in the process of the gunman securing money from the safe, coins and other things from the safe were scattered all over the floor, creating a very messy scene. I discovered this trigger later in life when I had my own home and guests would come to stay. In instances where the belongings of guests were scattered throughout the house, I became extremely anxious. I was by no means a "neat freak," so it was not related to needing to have everything in order—I certainly did my own scattering of personal belongings. Through counseling, I discovered that the trigger was the mess being caused by the outside—people coming into the house—just as the gunman did that night coming in McDonald's. These feelings became further intensified when I was unsure of how long someone would be staying, relating back to that time of waiting in the refrigerator, wondering when the nightmare would end. I still experience these powerful triggers more than forty years later.

I went to many counselors throughout the forty-year period. Most of the time, other issues in my life prompted me to seek counseling, but inevitably it came back to some aspect of the trauma that was still impacting my life. At one point, I went to a counselor that used the technique of eye movement desensitization and reprocessing (EMDR), which was a new treatment for trauma in the in the late 1980s and early 1990s. This treatment involved reliving the traumatic experience, describing what took place that night, while the therapist redirected my eye movements. As a new treatment for posttraumatic stress syndrome (PTSD), the premise was that anxiety about traumatic events was reduced when individuals were taught to engage in controlled eye movement. Although that technique and other forms of therapy gave me momentary relief, the trauma continued to affect me in a variety of ways and paralyzed my life on and off for many years.

Despite the ongoing emotional side effects, by the early 2000s, I was in a loving long-term relationship, I had obtained my doctoral degree and was teaching at North Central College in Naperville,

Illinois, preparing future teachers. My faith was deepening, and I was regularly attending mass. I no longer had the fear and racist beliefs that had strangled me in the early years following the tragedy at McDonald's. In fact, I had developed a passion for and focus on advocating for equity and diversity issues in my teaching and preparation of future teachers. I had also finally reached the point where I felt like I could "manage" the trauma. I learned to use strategies such as avoiding situations where I was in closed places, sitting in spaces in restaurants that face the door, and using calming techniques when visitors came to stay at our house, and these strategies were successful most of the time. However, I still felt that trauma was buried deep down inside, and I had to keep it contained. It felt like a rage boiling below the surface just waiting to explode if I were exposed to the right trigger. I knew I had to keep it contained for fear of how it could turn my life upside down again.

CHAPTER 4

—— ⟡ ——

Reconnecting with the Gunman

The beautiful thing about God is that He knows what we need and when we need it. I had become content with managing the trauma, hoping that it would never again surface its ugly head. I was content being a good Christian because I was attending weekly mass. Overall, life was moving along just fine, and I was living a relatively comfortable and happy life. In the spring of 2018, God decided to blow up my content and comfortable life, and He changed its course. One day out of the blue, I started thinking *I should really tell him that I forgive him.* I also found myself feeling empathy for him—he has been in prison for forty years; he was only nineteen years old, and now he is almost sixty years old. My heart was actually hurting for him. What in the world is happening? How could I possibly be feeling these things about a man who murdered my friend and made my life a living hell for so many years? But I was—there was no denying it.

Father Mark Bernhard, one of the priests at my church said in one of his homilies, "God is relentlessly pursuing you and me." The moment he said that, I realized that God was indeed relentlessly pursuing me. Shortly after this Epiphany in January 2019, I heard about a program at our church called Alpha, and my partner and I decided to attend because we had a desire to get to know more parishioners, and we wanted to deepen our faith. Alpha is a video-based, small group program, which covers all aspects of the Christian faith. Each week, all enrolled in the program gathered for a meal and watched a video covering a specific aspect of the Christian faith, followed by small group discussions. The Alpha group to which I was assigned provided me with the love and support I needed at that point. As I struggled with all of the conflicting emotions that were running through my mind and contemplated contacting the man who had caused such great pain in my life, support was definitely what I needed. In one of the sessions that focused on the need for forgiveness, I opened up and shared my story with the group. I was overwhelmed with the level of support I received from my Alpha brothers and sisters, affirming my desire to let him know of my forgiveness.

Not long after Alpha ended, we also attended the Christ Renews His Parish (CRHP) retreat weekend at the church. CRHP is a Catholic spiritual renewal program, which has been in existence since 1969. Participants spend the weekend engaged in prayer, praise, and several of the sacraments. One of the most powerful components of the CRHP weekend was hearing witness talks from the team providing the retreat, followed by discussion questions in small groups. Hearing how other women had overcome struggles and trauma through the grace of God was truly inspiring. Throughout the weekend, I was surrounded by loving and caring women who guided me through prayer, praise, and worship, and who continue to support me today. I have no doubt that both of these ministries (Alpha and CRHP) were the result of our Heavenly Father's way of surrounding me with His love and support as I would begin to embark upon the most important act of my life to date. The love and support from my Alpha team and my CRHP sisters was overwhelming, and it helped to build my courage to pursue what God had put in my heart.

I can do everything through Christ, who gives me strength. (Philippians 4:13)

After ALPHA ended and the CRHP weekend was over, I continued to *think* about writing the letter. However, I was faced with a busy time of the academic year with our trimester ending, and I chalked it up to not having time, but it was always in the back of my mind. We took a spring break trip to St. George, Utah—that would be a perfect time to write this letter. Prior to leaving for the trip, I spent time reading and marking scripture on forgiveness in my Bible. Being an inexperienced Bible reader, I turned to Google to search for appropriate scripture and added post-it notes in each section of my Bible for quick reference once I began writing. I had never referred to the Bible to write anything, but I knew that it was a must in this situation.

Once I was in St. George, I found one activity after another to avoid writing this letter. It was on one of my last full days of the trip that I finally gathered up the strength to tackle this challenging task, so I took my Bible and my pad of paper and headed out to a beautiful spot near our rental house. I climbed up on the pristine red rocks to write the letter amidst the beauty of God's work. As I made my way up to this beautiful spot, it began to rain! That could have been a really good excuse for me to avoid this task yet one more day, but I knew I needed to forge ahead because we would be leaving in one day, and I had vowed to write the letter while on this trip. So I climbed up on the rocks, found a little cave to sit in so I would not get soaked, and I prayed and wrote. As the rain fell, so did my tears, and I poured onto that paper forty years of pain, suffering, and forgiveness to a man whom I had never spoken—a man who upended my life—a man for whom I once had deep hatred.

Great, the letter was written, so I could go home, give it a final read, and send it. Well, that did not exactly happen. Once again, I had the excuse that I had to start my third trimester of the academic year, and then the trimester began to get very busy, and before I knew it, the academic year was over. The letter was always on my mind, but for some reason, I just could not bring myself to finalize and send it. When the academic year ended, I started going to daily mass where I prayed about the unfinished letter, and finally on the July 16, I finished it. As I finalized it, I decided that I wanted to give him an opportunity to respond if he chose, but I did not want to give him my home address for obvious reasons. Again, I started to question myself. Why would you want to hear anything back from this man? Just send the letter and be done with it. Needless to say, with God's relentless pursuit, I would give him the opportunity to write back. At the advice of a friend of mine who is a police officer, I asked if I could use the address of our church. The secretary of the church office was a member of my CRHP team, and she did not hesitate to tell me yes, as she was the person who received the mail each day.

When the letter was ready (Appendix A), I also addressed a small envelope to me with the return address of *Our Lady of Mercy*, put a stamp on it, and added it to the envelope in which I put his letter. I delivered the envelope to the post office, and I will never forget the feeling I had as I dropped that envelope into the post office mailbox. Once I let go, there was no way to get it back! Why in the world are you doing this? Do you really think it is going to make a difference? I truly had no idea what was to come and how I would respond if I heard nothing from him. Or for that matter, how I would respond if I did hear from him and he was not remorseful. As I waited, I started to wonder why I had set myself up for a potential hateful or ambivalent response, or no response at all for that matter. However, deep down inside, something told me that it was all going to be fine.

Now faith is the assurance of things hoped for,
the conviction of things not seen. (Hebrews 11:1)

July 16, 2019

Peter,

I am one of the six women who were in the McDonald's in Oak Forest November 29, 1979 when you robbed the store and killed my friend, Laura. I am writing to tell you that I forgive you. I hope this means something to you, as I am not writing this for me--this is not part of therapy, which is what one could think. Rather, I am writing this for you, Peter. I forgave you many years ago but recently, a thought popped into my mind that I should tell you. I believe that was God/Jesus letting me know that you deserve to know that at least one of us forgives you.

It has been a forty-year journey for me with emotions ranging from complete hatred of you to my current feelings of empathy for you. My journey has been very difficult but, with the help of God, I now can see beyond my own experience and needs to how difficult this has had to be on you. As a nineteen-year-old young man, I now know you made a mistake—a big mistake—one that has resulted in you living your life in the prison system, which I know cannot be easy. I am sorry for that—I truly am.

I don't know what life has been like for you all these years after the crime you committed—maybe you don't even ever think about that night or us. But if there are some remnants of memories and any guilt, I pray that hearing from at least one of us that you are forgiven will bring you peace, Peter. I also pray that you have asked God for forgiveness, as he is merciful and forgives all who ask, no matter what the sin.

You may not care at this point about hearing from any of us, but I wanted to write in case it is important for you to hear this—I forgive you, Peter. I know some people find God/Jesus in prison—I pray you are one of those people. If not, there is still time. God can bring you peace and mercy if you ask for guidance and forgiveness, Peter. *"If we confess our sins, He is faithful and just to forgive us our sins and to cleanse us from all unrighteousness."* 1 John 1:9.

See Appendix A for Maureen's full first letter

Less than two weeks later, I received an e-mail and voice message that I had a "special letter" in the church office. My heart sank—I was both nervous and excited. Needless to say, I went over to the office as soon as I had a break in my workday. When I walked in, my heart pounding, Diane held up an envelope, not the little one I had put in with my letter to him, but rather a big envelope—11 × 14! What could he possibly be sending me in such a large envelope?

My heart pounding, I took the envelope and went into the church. This was a moment for which I had waited forty years—a response that I never thought I would get—a response from the man who caused so much heartache, trauma, and grief in my life and in the lives of so many others that night. As I opened the envelope, in it I found many copies of certificates and recognition awards that he had received during his incarceration, mostly connected to ministry work he had been doing in the prison. I flipped through the pages one by one, tears flowing from my eyes. Also included was a copy of the associate degree in religion that he earned while in prison. I sat there in amazement, and I felt an instant sense of relief—he had found God. As I paged through it all, I came to his letter—it was five pages, handwritten! (Appendix B) As I read it, I wept, mostly tears of joy, as he explained how he was born again in 1997 and how he has been committed to serving our Heavenly Father through ministering the Word to others ever since then. He also expressed how remorseful he was for all of the pain and fear he had created in my life and all of those present that night, as well as the pain and grief he caused Laura's family. It appeared from the letter that this was a man who had devoted himself to the Lord and was expressing sincere remorse for his crime. It was clearly evident that he was truly grateful for my expression of forgiveness and for the grace and mercy that God had bestowed on him through this act of forgiveness. With all that said, I had some skepticism. What if this was an act, a way to manipulate me into thinking he was a changed man?

7-28-19.

Maureen,

 I truly thank you for taking time to write me a heart felt letter letting me know that you forgave me for the crimes I committed 40 years ago. I am very sorry for all the pain, hurt, heartache, mental and emotional anguish I caused the ▮▮▮▮ family, love ones, friends and co-workers who were very near and dear to Laura ▮▮▮▮.

 Your letter was the answer to our prayers. It came from the heart and touch our hearts and caused us to weep, giving thanks and praises to God. Most definitely an act of God's Spirit working in you both to will and to do of His good pleasures. Maureen it's no doubt God's work has been done! Thank you so very much for forgiven me. And I am very sorry for everything that you had to go through in the last 40 years over the loss of your dear friend and co-worker Laura ▮▮▮▮.

 Thank you for allowing God to help you to persevere through your 40 year journey of emotional rage and hatred of me to your current feelings of empathy for me.

See Appendix B for Peter's full first letter

After sitting in the church for quite a while, I went out to my car and sat some more and reread parts of the letter. I was in amazement with what I had received. Was this really happening? Had I just received an apology from the man who caused me forty years of pain and trauma? I was completely stunned. I was not even sure how to process what was happening—it seemed surreal. In the days that followed, I found myself wavering between complete joy and skepticism and doubt. Was this man really reformed, or did he just go through some programs while incarcerated to increase his chances for clemency? I experienced doubt about whether or not I was doing the right thing, but I was also very happy that I had what seemed like closure after all these years. I sent the letter, I received one back from him expressing great remorse, I did my duty as a Christian, and the cycle was complete, right? Wrong! God was not going to let it all end there. Even though I had doubt, I knew right away what I needed to do—I needed to ask if I could visit him in prison.

> *To whom much is given, much is required.*
> (Luke 12:48)

When I wrote the first letter, I wrote it in a pretty generic manner, with little to no expectations. I downplayed my faith, indicating that I was not a "Jesus freak," in case he had not found God. When his first letter clearly confirmed he was committed to the Lord, I wrote him a second letter (Appendix C), letting him know how happy I was to hear that he had devoted his life to God and asked if I could come and visit him. I also indicated that if it were not a good time for him to have this visit, it could happen later when he was ready. Before I knew it, we had paperwork completed and a date set for the visit—October 5. What in the world was I doing?! I think the human side of me rationalized that I needed to go see him so I could verify that he truly was remorseful and living a life devoted to Christ. However, I could not help but believe that God had something else in mind—something much bigger.

> *Trust in the LORD with all your heart, and do*
> *not rely on your own understanding.* (Proverbs 3:5)

August 9, 2019

Dear Peter,

When I received an email from the church secretary that I had a letter to pick up, my heart sank and I was filled with both nervousness and excitement, as I wasn't sure I would hear back from you. When I went to pick it up at the office and saw that the envelope was big and that it was obviously filled with more than just a letter, I was overwhelmed. I took it into the church and as I saw all the documentation of what you have done to better yourself and to give praise to Our Lord and Savior, I felt a huge sense of relief, knowing that you found God and have been doing so much to show your devotion to His Son by reading The Word and teaching others about the tremendous love of Our Father and His Son. Then I read your letter and just wept—with joy and with sadness. Joy that my letter touched your heart and was a sign of God's true love, because it truly was—God let me know that it was important for me to tell you that I forgave you. I also wept with sadness that you have had to live all of these years incarcerated.

I am so happy you have asked for God's forgiveness and He has given you such strength to endure these 40 years in the prison system and more importantly, the strength to help others in the prison system to see hope and have faith in the Greatness of Our Heavenly Father! The excerpt from the letter from Mike Frizzell and the other documents that show your participation in biblical studies/programs, as well as a degree in Theology studies are truly a testament to the work you have done to come closer to Jesus, study His Word and to help others in the prison system do the same. And your expressed desire to help schools, communities, neighborhoods, etc. to help "hopeless youth" is no doubt sincere. Praise God for his work through you, Peter!! You had a choice in how you handled your life in prison, and you chose GOD.

See Appendix C for Maureen's full second letter

As I waited for the visit, I shared my story with close friends and the men and women in my two church groups and received overwhelming encouragement and support, and I continued to pray. Then one day, when I shared the story with one of my closest friends, she asked me the question, "What do you hope to achieve by this visit?" Wow, that stopped me in my tracks. I had no idea how to even answer that. What *did* I hope to accomplish through this visit? I don't even remember what I said to Nancy in response to that question, but I do remember thinking that even though I couldn't really answer that question, I felt a very strong desire to make that visit. I knew the Holy Spirit was working in me.

> *Blessed are those who trust in the Lord and have made the Lord their hope and confidence.* (Jeremiah 17:7)

Before the visit, I had also spoken to several people in his life that he asked me to call in his second letter (Appendix D). He never really told me why he wanted me to call these people, but I assumed he wanted me to get validation regarding the changes he had made in his life, so I made the calls. The first person I called was his oldest sister, Crystal. After she expressed her extreme gratitude for my act of forgiveness, we had a wonderful conversation, and I felt an immediate comfort level and connection with her. Crystal shared briefly about his childhood, and then she discussed the challenging process that they had been through when petitioning for clemency several times during his incarceration. She also assured me that he was not the same man who committed that crime forty years ago—rather that he was a kind, caring, and gentle man. While I could feel the sincerity in her voice, I could not help but wonder if these were just words of a sister who desperately wanted to help her brother.

8.18.19

(i) Greetings, My Beloved Sister in Christ, Maureen

I pray this letter find you at your best in health, spirit and in a peaceful state of mind. As of myself, all is truly well and peaceful at this stage in my life. I am exceedingly glad with the fullness of joy because of you. Once again was I touch by your letter and the love of God that exude from your heart. My Beloved Sister in Christ, you are most definitely spirit filled and has been blessed with the spirit of discernment, who can share the letters I wrote you with anyone your heart desire. I know that you are truly lead and guided by the Spirit of God and you have my best interest at heart. Also I would love to behold the Physical Manifestation of a blessing and the miracle working of power of God with you on a visit. That may be the best of the first day of His purpose in our lives. I have enclosed a visiting list for you to complete and send back to me so I can mail it in to get approved

See Appendix D for Peter's full second letter

35

There was one bit of information that Crystal shared that struck a huge chord and shook me to my core. When I asked questions about his clemency hearings, she spoke about his recent hearing where Laura's family members spoke against clemency and stated that they believed his "clemency" was that he did not receive the death penalty forty years ago. I felt an immediate sense of guilt and sadness, thinking about how very difficult life must still be for Laura's family. Knowing the level of trauma and grief I suffered, I could not even imagine the depths of their grief. After I spoke with Crystal, those uneasy feelings remained with me.

I also spoke with several other people who he had asked me to contact, including a volunteer state chaplain at Pontiac Correctional Center, a retired correctional lieutenant from Pontiac Correctional Center, and a wrongfully convicted inmate who was released in April 2019, all of whom spoke confidently about the devotion to the Lord that he had developed during his incarceration and how he positively impacted their faith lives. With each call that I made, I was overcome with emotion, and I actually had to put distance between each call because it became so overwhelming—I could not believe that God had brought me to the point of forgiveness after all of these years.

Before the visit, I received several more letters, all filled with gratitude for my act of forgiveness and for my continued contact with him, including the upcoming visit. However, what I was most struck with was that his letters included a very unique style of incorporating scripture throughout. He was not just quoting scripture but using scripture to communicate his thoughts and feelings. For example, in one of his early letters, he wrote, "I agree, my sister in Christ, only God knows the Way that we will take and after we have been tried and tested, we shall come forth as pure gold. This will be an amazing journey by far and the best is yet to come, to God be the Glory!" Since those early letters, I have received hundreds of letters and notes through a phone app that contain this beautiful writing style, offering praise to God and prayers for my life.

For forty years, I referred to the man who killed my friend and brought terror into my life as "him," "the man," "the man who killed my friend." For any Harry Potter fans, it was kind of like Voldemort,

"He Who Shall Not be Named." I could not call him by name because that would humanize him. However, a shift occurred as I got to know him through his letters and through conversations with his sister, and I began calling him by his name—Peter. I believe this shift occurred before I met him because his letters communicated an incredible level of gratitude for my act of forgiveness and also a genuine and deep love for the Lord. In one letter, Peter wrote, "My heart is overwhelmed with joy unspeakable from the tears I continue to sow as a result of God's love working through you at this time and season in my life. God's amazing love from above can touch the heart of anyone that's alive on this earth; the best feeling anyone can experience in life." The man now had a name—Peter—and he would soon have a face.

CHAPTER 5

The First Prison Visit

From the time the date for the prison visit was determined, to the day of the visit was close to a month, it seemed so far away at first, and then the time just flew by, as time tends to do. When the week of the visit was upon me, my stress and anxiety levels began to increase, my chest was tight, my mind was whirling, and my emotions were running wild. I prayed regularly, asking God to please guide me through the visit and to give me the strength to face this man. That was one long week, and Saturday could not come quickly enough. I began questioning whether or not this was the right thing to do, even though I knew in my heart that this was truly God's will, and I needed to trust that it would be a good visit. Despite all of my hesitation and questioning, there was no point at which I ever considered the option of not going—I fully believed that God would not send me on this part of the journey for it to be a bad experience. This was the first time in my life that I had ever experienced this level of faith.

> *For we walk by faith, not by sight.* (2 Corinthians 5:7)

The day of the visit had arrived! To add more stress, it was a two-and-a-half-hour drive to the prison, so I had another two and a half hours to think about the visit. On top of that, I had never been to a prison before, so there was also that added stress and uncertainty. I was grateful that my partner was going with me, as I cannot even imagine going by myself.

> *Be strong and of good courage, do not fear or*
> *be in dread of them: for it is the Lord your God who*
> *goes with you; he will not fail you or forsake you.*
> (Deuteronomy 31:6)

During the drive, I thought listening to some of Pastor Rick Warren's *Daily Devotion* podcasts would be calming. I had only just recently subscribed to his daily devotion and was not yet a regular listener of the series, so I randomly selected one. I do not remember the title of the series I selected, but all three of the podcasts in the series referenced scripture from the New Testament that Paul wrote while imprisoned. Pastor Rick referenced how Paul spread the Word of God to the hundreds of guards he was chained to that rotated in to watch over him, as well as visitors that came to see him. I do not believe it was a coincidence that this series was randomly selected for my drive, where I would meet the man who also appeared to be doing ministry from the confines of prison. God knows what we need and when we need it, and He surely provided it that morning as I made the two-and-a-half-hour drive listening to that podcast.

Pulling into the parking lot of the prison, I looked at the ominous structure in front of me and paused, again, thinking, *What am I doing?* Before going in, we bowed our heads in prayer, and I asked for God to send the Holy Spirit through both me and Peter, allowing us to have a conversation that was honest, caring, and compassionate. As I approached the building, I was filled with anxiety, not only about the meeting, but about the fact that I was entering a foreign place and did not know the procedures. The guard who assisted us was very kind and explained the process. Once we were checked in, we had to go through a search, a metal detector, and were led to an area where our hands were stamped with an invisible stamp that we had to put under a scanner both on the way in and out. We then passed through several locked doors, the final of which was the type of door that we see on TV and in movies—the sliding door that goes really slow and has a deafening sound when it reaches the closing spot. That sound represented the sharp separation between freedom and imprisonment, and I could not imagine what life behind that door was like.

We were eventually taken to a room where there were inmates sitting at tables with family and friends, and we were assigned a table where we waited for Peter to come in. I had done a search online in the inmate database, so I knew generally what he looked like, which was very different than he did forty years ago, something for which I was grateful. I had already discussed with my partner what an appropriate greeting would be and had decided I would shake his hand. That seemed suitable for the situation. After what seemed like forever, I saw him enter the room and our eyes met. He made a head/eye gesture, silently asking, "Is that you?" and I nodded. As he approached, I heard him say I'm sorry, I'm sorry, I'm so very sorry, and he just kept repeating it. I broke down, sobbing, and as God would have it, there was no handshake that would take place—my instincts took over, and I reached up for a hug and we embraced, and he just kept saying how sorry he was with such sincerity that I truly felt the love of God embracing me. I wept, not with sadness, but with joy and gratitude. I was finally able to hear from him that he was sorry for the torment and grief he caused us forty years ago and for taking the life of Laura. Peter apologized in his letters, but I did not realize until that moment how badly I needed to hear those words from his mouth.

Our visit lasted more than two hours, as we talked about many things, the first of which had to be that night. I had let Peter know in one of my letters that I would need to talk to him about that night and that it was going to likely be very emotional for me. Knowing that, he came in with a bunch of paper towels so that I would have a way to wipe away my tears. I wanted to know why he shot her. What did he remember? I quickly learned that he did not remember much of anything. When I told him I was the first person he came to from behind, he looked both surprised and horrified. I explained to him what he did, gathering each of us up in the same place, and that Laura and another girl were the last ones that he brought over. Everyone was cooperating, so why did he shoot her? Peter said he has no idea why the gun went off—as he recalls, he had his finger on the trigger, but he did not know why it fired. He recalled that he was heavily under the influence of drugs and alcohol, and all of that likely clouded his actions and memories of that night.

This part of our conversation confirmed what I wondered for many years. Peter did not specifically target Laura; it was simply an accidental discharge of the gun. I have told the story of what happened that night to a number of friends and family over the years, and each one inevitably asks at some point in the story, why did he shoot her? My response has always been, I have no idea—we had all cooperated, no one panicked, the manager talked in a calm voice the whole time and assured him she would get him the money he came for. In the early years, I was convinced he murdered her intentionally, but it never made sense based on what happened that night. In recent years, it became apparent to me that it had to have been an accident—a really bad accident. Deep down inside I knew this, and I believe that is why I began to feel empathy toward Peter. He was a nineteen-year-old kid who made a really stupid mistake—mixing drugs, alcohol, and the use of a gun—a mistake that took the life of a beautiful human being, and it was a mistake that could not be corrected. He was paying for that mistake with his life, a life in prison. By no means am I making an excuse for his behavior, but knowing that her murder was not a part of the plan—it was a dreadful mistake, as a result of poor decisions, his age, his life circumstances—all of this has helped me in my forgiveness journey.

As we talked about family, prison life, my work, and other topics, I did not see the same man who came in and terrorized us, shot and killed Laura, put us all in the refrigerator, and held a gun to the head of the manager counting as he demanded she open the safe. That is not the man that sat before me, speaking verses from the Bible, and praising God for his life, even though he has been incarcerated for forty years. Rather, this was a kind, caring, and compassionate God-loving man who shared his genuine gratitude for my forgiveness and for my visit that day, as well as his genuine sorrow for the painful consequences of his crime.

When the time came to leave, Peter had to stay at the table, and we had to go to an area by the door and wait for the other inmate family members that would be leaving at the same time. As we were waiting, I will never forget the sad look in his eyes as he sat on the bench waving goodbye to us, a childlike face that just broke my heart to leave behind. Tears flowing abundantly, I looked back several times as I waited for the guard to open the door that led us out of the room. I did not really know this man, but I felt like I had known him all my life. In fact, after we left, my partner and I talked about the fact that it felt like we were just sitting with a friend we had known for years. How could it be that I am sad to leave behind a man who caused the greatest trauma in my life and took from this earth a beautiful human being? There is no other explanation but the love of God working in me. I knew that I would be back, and that this was by no means the end of this relationship.

Still slightly skeptical about the genuineness of Peter's remorse and commitment to God, I knew that I needed to continue communicating with him. After all, how could I turn my back on what God had made possible in my life? Shortly after the visit, I was added to his approved phone list so that we could talk on the phone. There is also a phone app that allows for communication with inmates, and I was also added as a connection to his contact list for that app. This has allowed us to send text messages to one another. It is through our phone calls and text messages, in addition to the additional prison visits I was able to make before the COVID-19 lockdown that I came to know Peter, a true disciple of Jesus.

CHAPTER 6

Conflicting Feelings

In one of his podcasts, Pastor Rick Warren talks about six things we should ask ourselves when making a major decision. One of these questions is, what is the cost? If we make a given decision, what are the potential negative outcomes that could come from it? Answering this question became a struggle for me shortly after I received Peter's second letter and continues to be to this day. After receiving Peter's second letter, I experienced emotions ranging from complete joy that I had been able to reach full forgiveness to complete guilt and worry that through my act of forgiveness I was somehow dishonoring Laura and her family. While these contradicting feelings still arise, I have to come back to God's will—what does He expect of me as His child?

When I initially forgave Peter years ago, I never felt guilt because it just seemed like the right thing to do to let go of the anger that was holding me back. I had not told many people about it; I was just able to somehow let go of the anger and anguish that plagued me. I question now whether this was really forgiveness or just releasing the anger and other emotions so that I could move on with a more positive outlook on life and no longer let the trauma rule my life. At any rate, it did make life a bit easier, and I was able to experience life in a more positive way. But there were always those deep, deep emotions that I suppressed and managed to contain below the surface—those feelings of fear and rage—that I had to contain to ensure that they did not surface and send me off the deep end.

In 2018, when God put in my heart that I needed to *tell* Peter that I had forgiven him, these thoughts truly came out of nowhere, and I have no doubt it was guidance from God. Why it took almost forty years, I have no idea, but forty is a very significant number in biblical history. Moses and the Israelites spent forty years wandering in the desert for a trip that should have taken two weeks because of their lack of trust in God. Perhaps my lack of trust in God is why it took so long. I am just glad He didn't make me wander in the desert for those forty years! Although I suppose I was wandering in the desert in a sense—thirsty for a true relationship with Jesus. Whatever the reason for the length of time it took, in 2018, God was clearly telling me I needed to contact Peter and let him know that I forgave him.

This was no surprise, as our God is a God of mercy and second (and third, and fourth, etc.) chances. Our Lord's prayer states, "forgive us our trespasses as we forgive those who trespass against us." God sent His only son to live among us to endure severe torture, and to die so that our sins could be forgiven. *Forgiveness* is mentioned fourteen times, and *forgive* is mentioned seventy-five times in the Bible. *Mercy* and *compassion* are mentioned hundreds of times. Who am I to decide not to forgive this man when God gave up His only Son for my sins and He forgives Peter? Although I did not realize this at the time, the only way I would reach full forgiveness was to tell Peter—I believe that was God's plan.

God is love, and only He can bring about the kind of full healing that I have experienced. As I read in a Rick Warren devotional, "Only the power of God can replace hate with love and set you free from the bitterness that can grow from deep hurts." I am truly grateful for this blessing. As I was writing this chapter, I read an entry in *Our Daily Bread*, December–February 2019–20 that referred to "God-Sized Love." The author of that devotion, Sheridan Voysey, discussed Jesus's Sermon on the Mount and how He presents a standard of love that is beyond comparison. God-sized love calls us to embrace not only the worthy, but those we perceive as undeserving—love that blesses everyone.

It is because of God's forgiveness of our sins and His incredible love for us that I was able to let Peter know that I forgave him—he deserved to hear it after all these years. Some might say he deserves nothing for what he did that night, let alone hearing of my forgiveness. I do not believe that was my decision to make. God did not say forgive *some* people who trespass against us and that we should randomly decide who we will forgive and who we will not. He said, *"Take heed to yourselves. If your brother sins against you, rebuke him; and if he repents, forgive him"* (Luke 17:3). Peter is truly remorseful and continues to repent for this horrible sin he committed. He has not only repented, but he dedicated his life in prison for the past twenty years to learning God's Word so that he could help other prisoners and prison staff find Jesus in their lives. Additionally, if he were ever released, Peter stated that he has a desire to help young men in situations similar to his as a nineteen-year-old, so they do not make the same costly mistake he did.

Does all of this lessen the pain and loss of such a beautiful young woman? Of course not. I understand that some reading this may be cynical, questioning how genuine Peter's remorse and intent to help others really is. I am sure some may also judge me for forgiving him. While this weighs on me, I am confident that this is the path that God has set forth for me, and I must follow that path.

In addition to my visits to the prison, I have talked to Peter on the phone almost daily since our first visit October 5, 2019, with the exception of the period of time the prison was in complete lockdown during the COVID-19 epidemic. I also receive daily prayers from him through the phone app. I see in Peter a God-loving man who is fully devoted to his Lord and Savior and spreading the Good News. He has taught me so much about worship, prayer, and putting God first in my life, and for that I will be forever grateful.

Laura and I never talked religion, but we saw each other frequently at mass on Sundays. I have no doubt whatsoever that she was filled with the Holy Spirit. Her joy-filled spirit, that beautiful smile, and her genuine care for others clearly showed her love of God and His love for her. Although I only knew her a very short time, I have a hard time thinking that she would want me to hold hatred in my heart all these years. In fact, I believe the opposite—she would want me to fully forgive so that I can carry the joy in my spirit that she once carried here on earth and that she no doubt still carries in her life everlasting.

For forty years, I have visited Laura's gravesite several times a year, honoring her memory with holiday and birthday decorations and flowers. Many tears have been shed there, praying for her soul, apologizing that she was the one taken that night, and thanking her for helping me to survive life when I did not think I could. Afterall, Laura truly is the reason that I was able to pull myself out of misery—I was doing it for her because she was not given the chance to live a long life. In the beginning, this was the only way I could justify living on because of the severe survivor's guilt I suffered. I convinced myself that I must move on and do good in my life for her because she was not given that chance. On my cemetery visit Christmas, 2019, I "talked" to her about my journey of forgiveness, about Peter, and prayed that this is what she would want from me. Knowing the God-filled young woman she was here on earth, and no doubt is in heaven, I truly believe that she would bless my course of action.

With that said, I absolutely understand the extreme difficulty that Laura's family members may still face in arriving at full forgiveness. Their loss was so much deeper and more significant than mine—they lost their child, their sister, their cousin, and their niece. And the children that were born to her siblings were never able to meet their beloved aunt. I have prayed for them for years, hoping that each of them has found peace in their hearts and lives, knowing that Laura is with our Heavenly Father in eternal life. I have also prayed that they have been able to release some of the anger that may still consume them so that they can experience some of the joys of life. I will continue to pray for the family and the other women who were present that night, that they may come to full forgiveness so that they too they can experience the freedom that I now feel from the pain and suffering from that night.

> *Blessed are those who mourn, for they shall be comforted.* (Matthew 5:4)

I understand that my experience is very unique and that there are many victims of violent crimes whose experiences are vastly different. I am certain that there are many offenders of violent crimes who have not devoted themselves to God while in prison. My story would be very different if Peter had not fully committed his life to Jesus in 1997. Perhaps I would still visit him and communicate with him regularly, but I suspect the relationship would remain pretty superficial. This is the miraculous part of the story—God's love, grace, and mercy led to Peter's conversion, and forty years later, His love, grace, and mercy led me back to Peter so that both of us could be fully healed. It was all according to His time. If I had sent the letter when I first forgave Peter, the outcome would have probably been very different. There is no explanation other than God for this occurrence in my life.

For Everything there is a season, and a time for every matter under heaven. (Ecclesiastes 3:1)

CHAPTER 7

――― ∾ ―――

Peter's Spiritual Journey in Prison

After his sentencing in 1981, Peter was sent to Stateville Correctional Center in Joliet, Illinois. Over the course of his incarceration, he also did time in Pontiac and Menard Correctional Centers, both of which are also maximum-security prisons. He is currently in a medium-security prison. Entering the prison system as a nineteen-year-old was no doubt frightening and intimidating. He had to quickly learn how to survive in an environment that sometimes even rivaled the illegal activity that occurs in high-crime areas of the city. But with his street smarts, he quickly learned how to survive in a prison system that was very corrupt and influenced heavily by the gangs. Even though he was supported by his family, including his uncle Frank who was a minister, the prison environment provided very little support for spiritual growth in the early days of his incarceration. Rather than provide specifics about Peter's early time in prison, I have included a general description of the Illinois prison system in the 1980s and early 1990s that I gathered through newspaper articles to paint a picture of the environment he lived in as he entered the Illinois correctional system.

Throughout the 1980s and 1990s, criticism of the Illinois prison system was mounting. The media captured various incidents within the system, depicting corruption. For example, in 1991, in retaliation of a guard shooting of a gang member incarcerated in Stateville, inmates from the same gang kidnapped and held hostage three guards, and in a separate facility (Menard Correctional Center), another member of the same gang stabbed a guard when he was let out of his cell for lunch (*Chicago Tribune*, July 18, 1991). In 1996, a Chicago gang leader was federally charged with running a huge drug distribution network while he was in a state prison. These, and no doubt many other incidents, "raised concerns about the power of street-gang members within state prisons, and their ability to communicate and incite violence behind bars" (*Chicago Tribune*, July 18, 1991). Additionally, there had been regular accusations from prison guards that prison administrators negotiated prison policies with gang leaders (*Chicago Tribune*, July 18, 1991).

In 1996, the Illinois Department of Corrections faced a major scandal when a videotape of the mass murderer Richard Speck was made available. Speck had been given a death penalty sentence for raping, torturing, and murdering eight student nurses in 1966 in Chicago; however, the sentence was later commuted to eight consecutive terms of 50 to 150 years each. The video, which captured Speck snorting cocaine and conducting sexual acts with another prisoner, was shared with Chicago news reporter, Bill Kurtis. Speck was also seen flashing $100 bills, saying at one point, "If they only knew how much fun I was having in here, they would turn me loose" (*The New York Times*, May 16, 1996). The Speck video was the turning point in pushing Illinois lawmakers to do a thorough investigation into the Illinois Correctional System in an attempt to regain control of the prison operations.

I provided this information not to create sympathy for Peter but to paint a picture of the environment in which he spent the first two decades of his incarceration; an environment filled with drugs, gangs, and corruption. As a result of the Speck tape investigation and efforts for authorities to take back control of the prison environments, inmates were offered the option of protective custody. This provided inmates housing in a separate section of the prison, and Peter made the choice to do this. During those first two decades, he had regular conversations with his Uncle Frank, and he attended church services, but he was doing what Peter referred to as "playing church." He was not living the Word, as he was still involved in the illicit activity going on in the prison.

In 1997, one day when he was lying in his cell, Peter felt overcome by the Spirit of God, as he describes it. He indicated that it was such an intense feeling that he knew it was God speaking to him; he ended up on his knees. That day, he was supposed to be involved in a drug deal, one which he knew then he could not participate. When he told the other inmates, they were shocked that he was not going to go through with the deal and astonished at what they were hearing from him. His conversion was so dramatic that, for a period of time, many of the inmates thought he was "faking it." Peter's life changed on that day in 1997 when he committed himself to Jesus Christ and vowed to discontinue any activity that was not consistent with God's teachings. He devoted himself to studying and sharing the Word and the love of God with others.

After moving into protective custody, he was able to enroll in Bible studies and other programs to better himself. He also enrolled in a college program and received an associate degree in religion, which made his Uncle Frank so proud. He did not have to make these choices, as he could have stayed in the general population living area and could have continued to engage in illicit activities. However, after experiencing the Spirit of God through what he refers to as a miraculous conversion, Peter knew what he needed to do. He shared with me how this change affected his prison life, stating, "My conversion enabled me to become a model prisoner; someone trustworthy, honest, and steadfast! It kept me out of trouble and obedient." Peter regularly talks about how being a Christian is a lifestyle and that he needs to be fully committed to God's ways. He was diligent and fully invested in learning the Word of God because he "wanted to be filled with the knowledge of His Will in all wisdom and spiritual understanding." He began to devour the Word by reading the Bible and Christian books, listening to Christian TV and radio, and through fellowship with other believers. Peter said he could not get enough of God. He now refers to it as having a "hunger and thirst for righteousness" as described in Matthew 5:6. As he immersed himself in the Word, Peter's whole being changed, "I began to take on a spirit of humility and to be a faithful servant unto Him. I knew I needed to allow the Holy Spirit that was in me to guide and to lead me and to do the things that God would have me to do. One of the biggest things was trusting in Him, believing and relying on Him."

As a humble servant, Peter was naturally drawn to sharing the Word with others. Prison ministers and a fellow inmate that was his mentor validated his desire to serve God. Peter explained, "They were telling me this is God's calling for your life, and I began to let that take effect on my life because I knew I was in the will of God by doing what He was telling me to do." Thus, a natural extension of Peter's spiritual journey was the impact that he had on other inmates and prison employees. In order to examine that impact, I interviewed two former inmates, a former employee of the Illinois Department of Corrections and several prison ministers to get their perspective about Peter's character since his spiritual conversion. The common theme from those I interviewed is that Peter has grown to be a humble servant to others, devoted to Christ and always focused on bringing God's Word to all he encounters. He is described as a kind, caring, and compassionate man who has integrity and is honest and genuine.

A former employee of the Department of Corrections, Mike Frizzell spoke with passion about the fact that Peter inspired him to go into prison ministry after his retirement. He met Peter when he was working at Pontiac Correctional Center because another officer had told him about how Peter helped her to find Christ. Curious, Mike sought out Peter in his assignment to the officer's kitchen and began having daily conversations with him. Eventually, a friendship developed when Mike began doing prison ministry in 2011 after his retirement. Peter attended Mike's Bible study sessions, and they continued their fellowship and prayerful conversations. They had conversations about Peter's desire to be released to help others outside of the prison, and Mike told him, "God is using you where you are at— you're leading people to Christ with your testimony, with your life, and with your example." Mike indicated that "countless inmates were impacted by Pete." In a letter to support Peter's request for clemency in 2016, Mike indicated, "In the course of my thirty-year career in corrections, I learned two things: 1) the Department of Corrections does not 'correct' anyone; and 2) the only people (inmates and staff) in whom I have observed a genuine change in their behavior and lives are those who come to saving faith in Jesus Christ." He indicated that Peter is "one of the best examples I know of a changed man."

While interviewing four additional prison ministers, I learned more about Peter's involvement in the ministry services, his mentoring of other prisoners, and the deep faith he developed while incarcerated. Linda Weatherspoon, who has known Peter for over thirty years, indicated that she first met him because the guards told her about an inmate that was an incredible prayer warrior, so she sought him out. After meeting him, Peter started helping her with the chapel services, setting up the chapel and making sure everything was ready for the start of services. He also went from cell to cell, letting inmates know that services were going to be starting and inviting them to attend. Chuck and Barbara Smith, a married couple who do ministry together, also commented on how Peter worked with other inmates to help them understand scripture. Chuck remarked that "the work comes when you do your homework, when you study The Word during the week. And he would help those guys understand The Word through the week, which made them even more excited to come to service because they were growing in Christ. He was doing the work when we weren't there."

Another prison minister, Tony McNeal, indicated Peter was one of the first to step up and get involved in services and that once he did, that helped other inmates to come forward. Tony spoke of Peter's impact on other inmates, remarking, "To watch him grow, to teach, and be involved with other inmates for their best interest was a blessing to see. He had a great influence on other inmates. He helped them to grow and he was relevant with them and also challenged them." Tony also articulated the significant role that Peter played in the growth of ministry services, stating, that "he's a true inspiration to those incarcerated and those who serve as volunteers. He left an indelible mark on all of us. He's a great man to know, and I am honored to have met him."

Minister Dee Dee Osobor spoke of her initial meeting with Peter and the trust that was given to him by the guards, indicating, "I knew he was going to be special because, first of all, he was walking the gallery and I know you have to be trusted to walk the gallery. He was walking the gallery and I was doing cell by cell ministry." The gallery is the walkway between the cells. It is highly unusual that an inmate would be trusted to walk freely through the gallery. Because of the powerful first interaction Dee Dee had with Peter, she always sought him out. "When I would come back and we would go to that building, I would always look for Peter. His whole demeaner is so calm. He has this calmness and charismatic way about him—not like somebody who has been away from family and friends for so long—they can become bitter."

Each of the prison ministers that I spoke with not only talked about how he helped them and other inmates, but also spoke emphatically about his character and his commitment to God. Linda spoke about his discipline, which she indicated she does not see very often in inmates. "A lot of them couldn't do that. They would come to the service, but they could not discipline themselves. He was very disciplined. His heart said, 'I have to please God no matter where I am at.' He would study all the time. Peter has a stronger spiritual walk compared to a lot of those preaching on the pulpit. He is very strong in his faith. He is committed to God, he is dedicated to the work that He asks. A lot of the people I work with do not have that spiritual commitment, but he does."

Barbara Smith talked about Peter's gift of prayer, "Peter was unique. He could pray like nobody. He could pray even better than us ministers who came in. You could see that there was something special about him." Chuck Smith spoke of the admiration he and Barbara have for Peter, "We have the highest respect and love for Peter just like a spiritual brother. We just cannot say enough about him in his spiritual walk, as a man—he is a man of integrity and great character. Barbara and I have been in prison ministry over twenty-five years, and Peter is a person that we always hold up. We don't always say his name, but when people ask us 'do people really change who are incarcerated?' Peter is the first one that comes to our mind to say what God really can do. He's the guy that comes to my mind whenever we talk about a changed life."

Dee Dee also referenced Peter's character and spiritual development, indicating, "I have the pleasure to meet a lot of people in prison, and there are two that have stood out to me, Peter is one of them. It is one thing to be in church with your average believer, but Peter wanted to get into the Holy of Holy. His desire was to go 'beyond the veil.' I feel that Peter has had that type of encounter with God. Whereas the average believer, we go to church, we give our lives to Christ, serve on an auxiliary, we pay our tithes, and that's the extent of it. He would be dangerous on the street because he would put the average preacher to shame."

Linda's testimony of Peter's character and commitment to God mirrored the above testimony, when she indicated, "In all of my years of prison ministry, I have never spoken for an inmate, gone to their clemency hearing; I have never done any of that, but I went with Peter because he is for real. Three things happen when you are in prison ministry that you find. You find lies, manipulation, and deceit. And he is none of those. He is so honest and sincere. He does not pretend to be something that he is not. If he tells you he is going to pray for you, trust me, he is going to pray for you. He is real about his prayer. He is that example, that they can use as a model for other prisoners—if you want to get out, this is the type of person you need to become."

In addition to the correctional officer and prison ministers, I spoke with two former inmates about their perceptions of Peter. Joe Hart described Peter as "a guy that was a servant to others, he was extremely humble." He attended church services with Peter, and they prayed together. Joe described a powerful interaction when Peter came to his cell exactly four years to the date on which he committed the robbery that led to his incarceration. Not knowing of the significance of the date, Peter told him that there would be a special church service that day and that Joe should go to it. Later that morning, Joe was awakened to an announcement that a service was starting in the chapel, and he went. At the end of the service, the minister was talking to many of the inmates individually, and when she came to Joe, she told him that God had something special in store for him, resulting in a spiritual awakening for him. Joe was released from prison in 2000, and on December 20, 2002, he drove by the same business that he robbed and saw two guys robbing it exactly seven years from the date of his robbery. Joe was able to stop the robbery, putting his own life in danger. Some would say this is coincidence, but I believe that this is divine intervention. Joe expressed his gratitude for the role that Peter played in serving his fellow inmates remarking, "He has suffered. I can say this personally, and it breaks my heart. He got himself there, and at the same time, he had a wonderful experience; he came to acceptance that 'this is my purpose, I'm going to serve others.'"

My interview with James Gibson revealed the most powerful impact of Peter in his ministry to other inmates. James was wrongfully accused and convicted of a double murder and incarcerated for twenty-nine years. In 2019, he was exonerated and released. As one can imagine, James entered the system very bitter, filled with resentment, and was very confused. James frequently went to the location where church services were held in the prison, but he never entered the chapel. One day in 1992, Peter approached him and urged him to come in for services, but James indicated he was not ready for that. For years, even before Peter's full conversion, James watched him moving around the cell houses preaching the Word and in the chapel as he was singing, preaching, and asking brothers to come in. But he never spoke to Peter—he just watched him.

In 2005, an incident occurred where several inmates were accused of running an illegal operation, and Peter and James were two of the ten accused. When the investigations concluded, they were the only two that were proven innocent, and the incident brought the two of them together. One day when they were both in the yard, James heard Peter complaining to another guy about something, and James confronted him, asking "Your name is Peter Logan, right?" After Peter replied yes, James continued, "I been watching you for twenty years. You made me really feel bad because I look up to you for inspiration and as a religious figure, and now you are on the yard complaining. Don't you serve a God?" After Peter replied yes, he asked James the same question, and James indicated, "I don't serve nobody but myself." Peter then asked him if he prays, and James indicated that he did not know how and what to pray. Peter decided he would change that.

As they talked a bit more, Peter asked James if he could do something for him. After James questioned why he would want to do something for him, Peter responded, "If you would come to the yard for the next thirty days, I'm guaranteeing you that I can change your life. I'm going to write you a prayer, a different prayer every day for the next thirty days, and if I can't personally get it to you, I'm going to make sure that it is delivered to you every day." It is typical for inmates to offer to buy one another something from the commissary when favors are done. According to James, "He (Peter) said you don't have to buy me anything, you don't have to give me anything, all you have to do is give me five minutes of your time every day that you come on to the yard, and I'll have a different prayer for you." Expressing his profound gratitude to Peter, James remarked, "He wrote me a prayer starting in July 2005, and it ended in August, a different prayer each day. After those thirty days, I was forever changed. I was forever converted. I started going to the church in 2005, and I ain't missed a day. I still have those prayers that he wrote with his own handwriting in 2005 in my home, and I say those prayers to this day with my girlfriend. Those prayers forever changed my life. I have not been the same since. He forever changed my life by teaching me the power of prayer. I went to the Bible, and I read from Genesis to Revelation. I read a chapter a day, until I completed reading from front to back, and it transformed my life and my mind, and I have not been the same since."

After James was exonerated and released in April 2019, he discovered something about the prayers that Peter wrote for him. He had been praying them since 2005, but it was not until fourteen years later that he realized the significance of the content of the prayers. "I didn't really look at those prayers, *really* look at it and feel what I had been praying to God, and you know in every one of those prayers, it never asks for anything. All it did was say, I thank You. And when I went back and started reading the Word, it said if I put

God first and just tell Him thank You for whatever it may be, He will be with me. It never said, if You get me out of prison, I will do this, etc. It always just said thank You." James attributes his release and all that has happened to right the wrongs for him and others who were tortured into confessing to crimes they did not commit to the power of those prayers. "These prayers right here are so powerful that I will keep these prayers until the day I die."

When asked about Peter's faith and impact on other inmates, James remarked, "I heard about other lives Mr. Logan has changed and touched, and I can tell you first-hand that he has been a changed man and a faithful servant of the Lord for twenty years. He has been steadfast in the Word of God. He has touched and changed thousands of lives. And he is serious about that Word of God. I believe that God has been working through him like no other person I've ever seen."

For years, Peter has prayed for a second chance. He said he would frequently cry out to God, "I know that You are not going to let me spend the rest of my life in prison for something that You know I didn't intentionally do." He had three dreams, one in Statesville (1999) and two in Pontiac (2004 and 2005). After his dreams, eight other people had dreams of Peter being out in world. "I knew God was speaking to me. What are the chances that eight different people would have a dream that I was out in the world?" In his darkest season, he prayed regularly, "(I was) thanking Him for a miracle and thanking Him for my miracle, and then I received your letter, so I knew that it was God." Peter says that this was God communicating to him, "He was saying, son, I have not forgotten your labor of love and how you are ministering, so continue to do what you've been doing; your time is near."

I have personally witnessed that Peter is a changed man through my visits to the prison, and my ongoing phone conversations and text messages from him, which always include him praying for me and others. However, it was also validating to hear the consistent message from those who have interacted with him in the prison and have witnessed and benefitted from his ministry throughout the past twenty years. These testimonies provide ongoing and strong evidence of a changed man, but also evidence of a man who has gone to the highest levels of serving God for the benefit of others. While not dismissing his crime, one can acknowledge the good he has done with his life while incarcerated. There are many inmates who enter the system, get engrossed in the illicit activity that goes on in prison, or simply remain the same person they were when they entered the system. It is a choice to change, and Peter has obviously made the choice that we hope all inmates will make so that they can be truly reformed and repent for their crimes. Peter is definitely not the same man who committed those crimes back in 1979.

CHAPTER 8

My Spiritual Journey

In one of his podcasts, Pastor Rick Warren speaks about three responses we can have to a traumatic event in our life. We can let it *destroy us*, we can let it *define us*, or we can let it *develop us*. I have let the traumatic event in my life do all three of these things to me. Unfortunately, I did not allow it to develop me until decades later. It is my hope that, by describing my spiritual journey, I can help the victims of violent crimes who are reading this book to reach the point of allowing their trauma to develop them much sooner than I did.

In 1979, I wanted nothing to do with God, but I will tell you forty years later, God has been with me every step of the way, trying to get my attention, even as I turned my back on Him for many of those years. I was not scheduled to work at McDonald's that night in 1979, but that was part of God's plan for my life. Am I saying that God planned all aspects of that night? No, I am not. I do not believe that God planned for Laura to die that night. Laura died because Peter came into McDonald's with a loaded gun while high on drugs and alcohol. God gives us free will, and unfortunately, Peter made a choice that not only ended Laura's life, but altered the course of his life, the lives of all of that were there that night, as well as the lives of Laura's and Peter's family members. But my life today would be very different if I had not worked that night, and while I suffered immensely for years, I am convinced that I am a more humane, caring, and better person because of the grief and trauma that I suffered as a result of that night. God uses difficult situations to prepare us for what is coming in our lives. The impact of the bad choice Peter made that night is unimaginable unless you have been through something this traumatic. As a result of that night, I endured pain, fear, hate, and deep sorrow beyond any explanation, as I'm sure the rest of the women present did. Peter was sentenced to spend the rest of his life in prison. With that said, when something horrible happens in our lives, we have a choice on how we respond to it—we can let it destroy us, define us, or develop us. In my case, I made many poor choices along the way, but decades later, I began to let it develop me. As much as I did not want to hear that I needed God in my life to get me through the grief and trauma, I now know that God is the only way to full healing and forgiveness. I was not able to see this until I looked back forty years later.

God became central to my life in a slow and steady process. It did not happen all at once. I first started to reconnect with God when I began attending the Newman Center in DeKalb, Illinois while working at Northern Illinois University, and it brought me back to my Catholic roots. I previously attended the Newman Center sporadically as a college student; however, because of my extensive grief and the effects of the trauma, I did not attend mass on any kind of regular basis during my college years. In January 1994, I felt an overwhelming desire to return to the Newman Center, even though I was living twenty-five miles away at the time and had not attended mass there for over a decade. Perhaps it was because I had started reading books, which had a spiritual focus, as well as a focus on positive thinking. This helped me somewhat shift my thinking from being a victim to viewing myself as a survivor. Or perhaps there was another reason.

Although I was still feeling lost and hopeless, I immediately felt a sense of fellowship and an instantaneous renewal of my faith coming back this faith community. I began to focus on all that I had rather than all that I did not have. This was the beginning of my understanding of the power of gratitude. And in the process of this shift in my thinking, I learned of the importance of forgiveness so that I could truly move on with my life. I forgave the man who killed my friend and caused me so much pain and fear, and that really did allow me to experience more joy in my life.

In 1994, for the first time in my life, I began to feel the presence of God. One day in mass, I was overcome with an incredibly overwhelming emotion, and I found myself just sobbing—it was not really a sad sobbing, but I was not sure what was happening. I knew God was present, and I now know that He sent His Holy Spirit to fill me. I had never had such a feeling prior to this. After mass, I talked about this feeling with a friend and told her that I felt like I was given this blessing in order to help me deal with the death of someone close to me. Four months later, I would learn that my mom had stage 4 lung cancer. As I reflect back on that time, I know that God was filling me with the Holy Spirit to let me know He was there and to help me through the second most challenging time of my life.

My mom's diagnosis was the first time that I really started to pray regularly. My mom knew that her chances of beating the cancer were slim to none, and she immediately said that she did not want to get chemo treatments. It turned out that the cancer was so widespread that they could not have done chemo even if she agreed, but they did do radiation to shrink the tumors that had grown up and down her neck and spine. I saw how much agony and anguish this caused her, so I knew that I had to start praying. It was the hardest prayer I ever prayed, but I prayed each day—first, for a miracle—her full healing. Then second, if a miracle cure were not possible, that He would take her to His Heavenly Kingdom quickly.

> *Likewise, the Spirit helps us in our weakness;*
> *for we do not know how to pray as we ought, but the*
> *Spirit himself intercedes for us with sighs too deep*
> *for words.* (Romans 8:26)

The second part of my prayer was answered, and my mom passed on to life everlasting just two months after her diagnosis. My mom was the one who first connected me to the Catholic faith as a child, and it was only fitting that her death brought me back to the faith and our Heavenly Father knew just what I needed and when I needed it.

> *And my God will supply every need of yours*
> *according to his riches in glory in Christ Jesus.*
> (Philippians 4:19)

After my mom's death, I was lost once again. The death of a loved one often triggers grief from other losses; thus, my grief for the loss of Laura and the effects of the trauma intensified once again. Overwhelmed, I just could not imagine living the rest of my life without my mom. Then, Our Heavenly Father intervened on my behalf again. I secured my first full-time faculty position at a small Franciscan-based college.

> *For I know the plans I have for you, declares*
> *the Lord, plans for welfare and not for evil, to give*
> *you a future and a hope.* (Jeremiah 29:11)

I quickly found a sense of comfort and peace at this college, where the chapel was right down the hall from my office, and I had daily interactions with many of the Sisters of St. Francis who were teaching or working in offices at the college. Although I missed my mom terribly, as my faith continued to grow in this wonderful new environment, my heart began to heal, and the pain of the losses became more bearable. In my third year, the college began to experience increased financial problems, and as much as I loved it there, I knew that I had to start looking for another position. Additionally, I really wanted to move back to Illinois to be closer to my siblings and their children. Our Heavenly Father came through again. I was hired at North Central College in Naperville in 1998 and have been there ever since. This move is how I came to be connected to my current parish, Our Lady of Mercy, as my partner and I bought a house less than five minutes from the church.

> *Rejoice always, pray continually, give thanks*
> *in all circumstances; for this is God's will for you in*
> *Christ Jesus.* (1 Thessalonians 5:16–18)

Once I settled into life at North Central College, I quickly learned of God's next plan to bring me closer to Him. He blessed me with my colleague, Lora, who was a major factor in another huge shift in my life. Lora was a true disciple of Jesus—always joyful and seeing the good in everyone. She had a simple but powerful message that she was fond of sharing with faculty and her students—"nice matters." It is from Lora that I truly learned to have an attitude of gratitude. Several years into her time at North Central, she was diagnosed with stage 4 ovarian cancer and lived less than a year after diagnosis, but she never stopped talking about her gratitude for all the gifts that the Lord had given her, even on her worst days. Our Heavenly Father, once again, provided his loving care to me by putting Lora in my life to teach me the true meaning of gratitude and discipleship. I began praying daily, sometimes several times a day, always praising God for His love, presence, and grace in my life. I found peace in my heart and began to really see things differently—I began to see how truly blessed I was.

The other major influence in my spiritual development at this time was Joel and Victoria Osteen's daily devotion, *Today's Word*, which comes in the form of a daily e-mail. When I started reading these daily devotions, my entire way of thinking changed—especially my way of thinking about God. The Osteen's devotions focus on gratitude, hope, and praise. These messages combined with the deeper understanding of gratitude that I learned from Lora provided me with a more developed faith and understanding of the power of God. I continue to receive and read these daily devotions and listen to Joel's podcasts on Sirius Radio on a daily basis to fuel my spirit.

By 2012, I was continuing to grow in faith, and yet another challenging situation would arise in my life. My dad was diagnosed with stage 4 lung cancer. I immediately went to his house in San Antonio, Texas, and he informed me that he had two weeks to live. He had nothing to base this on, but he insisted that was his timeline. I knew I needed to get him back to Illinois so everyone could see him, and I was able to convince him pretty quickly to come to our house. Before we left Texas, he asked me to do something for him when he was no longer able to do it himself. He asked me to pray the Chaplet of the Divine Mercy. At the time, I did not know what this was, but I have come to know how very special this set of prayers is in the Catholic faith. Once we got him back to our house and he was surrounded by family, I continued to pray the Chaplet with him, and when he was no longer able to say it himself, I prayed it for him as he requested until he passed on to life everlasting. I have come to learn that my father, the one who only attended mass on Christmas and Easter most of my life, would teach me one of the greatest faith lessons in the importance of the Chaplet of the Divine Mercy to our Catholic faith. The chaplet was communicated to Sister, now Saint Faustina Kowalska, through visions and conversations with Jesus in the early 1900s. As a Catholic devotion, the Chaplet is said using the Rosary.

God blesses those who are merciful, for they will be shown mercy. (Matthew 5:7)

Although I didn't recognize it at the time, all of these situations and experiences were part of God's plan to bring me closer to Him so that I could finally fully understand how essential His presence in my life was and how important it was for me develop a relationship with Jesus. This would be critical as I prepared to do one of the hardest things in my life—contact that man who killed my friend and caused severe trauma in my life. Our Heavenly Father ensured I had the extra resources to go deeper in my relationship with Him and His Son by drawing me to the Alpha Program and the Christ Renews His Parish (CRHP) retreat weekend just at right at the time. For years, I had thought about participating in the CRHP weekend; in 2018, I had a very strong desire to sign up. Prior to doing the Alpha Program and participating in the CRHP weekend, the only time I had read the Bible was when I was searching for scripture to include in my parents' funeral services. As of the writing of this book, I am enrolled in my third Bible study, and I read the Bible almost every day. I have truly loved learning the history of our faith and the studying God's Word individually and in fellowship with my brothers and sisters in

Christ. God knew that He needed to take me deeper in my faith in order to prepare me for the final stage of my forgiveness journey.

I did not realize it at the time, but there was also a book that I read in the early 1990s that I believe laid a foundation for my change of heart. In 1993, Sister Helen Prejean wrote a book titled, *Dead Man Walking*, which tells the story of her ministry beginning in 1982 with a death row inmate, as well as her ministry with the victims' families. Through this ministry, she emerged as a staunch advocate against the death penalty and continues this activism to this day. Although Peter was not sentenced to death, I remember being very drawn to her book, and when I read it, I was in awe of her compassion toward a man who, with his brother, murdered a young couple after raping the female victim. She served as his spiritual advisor until his execution and showed such grace and mercy in her ministry to both him and the victims' families. My admiration for Sr. Helen continued throughout my life and resurfaced in recent years. I am grateful that God chose me to show His love and mercy to Peter forty years later and that he prepared me with such intent and purpose every step of the way.

My faith journey and my journey to full forgiveness has truly been an extraordinary experience. God's work to silently intervene on my behalf, putting me in the places I needed to be and with the people with which I needed to be over the past forty years, shows His unfailing love for me, even when I turned my back on Him for so many years. None of this would have been possible if I did not finally *let* Him lead me. While I had learned to deal with the trauma of my past, I never thought it could be possible to love the man who I once despised for killing my friend. God is the only explanation for this miracle. While I once viewed this as the last part of my long journey, I now know this is only the beginning to what God has in store for me.

Will I ever forget the horror of night and the tragic loss of Laura? Of course, I will not. Laura holds a special place in my heart, and I will always cherish that. I still grieve over the fact that I never got to know her as an adult, as I know she would have set the world on fire! I joyfully anticipate meeting her again when my life here on earth ends. However, as Saint Faustina said, mercy is the greatest attribute of God. As God is merciful, we too are called to be merciful. Peter is not the same man who entered the McDonald's in 1979. He is a devoted man of God, and I know this because he has become my spiritual mentor. In addition to his daily prayers, he has taught me how to pray using scripture and how to personalize scripture as I read it. During my visits to the prison, inevitably he sends me to the shelf in the visiting room to get a Bible after we have had a chance to catch up on happenings in each other's lives. Peter knows the Bible so well that he is able to quickly locate a verse that applies to something we are talking about and to explain its relevance. And he knows hundreds, if not thousands, of scripture verses by heart and recites them with a grace and beauty.

I typically visit Laura's gravesite on her birthday. In March 2020, I was not able to do so because I spent the winter months in Arizona. When I spoke with Peter that day, he offered up the following prayer to Laura and her family.

Heavenly Father, we are thankful for You sending the Holy Spirit to comfort Laura's family on their beloved daughter's birthday. We know You have blessed the family with so many precious memories they will cherish for a lifetime. Heavenly Father, Maureen and I thank You for blessing her family and keeping them and for being merciful and gracious to them and making Your face shine with pleasure upon them in a glorious way each and every day of their life here on earth. As they walk in the Light of Your countenance, give them Peace (tranquility of heart and life continually). We thank You for Your continual protection in the lives of this beloved family, and we thank You for the Holy Spirit that will continue to comfort, counsel, help, intercede, defend, strengthen, and stand by this family in the times of grief and sorrow. In Jesus's name, we pray. So Be It (Amen).

Peter rarely calls me by my given name but rather refers to me as Miracle. I am a very humble person, so this took a while for me to get used to, but I now know and honor what my presence in his life means to him. Not a day goes by that he does not either say or write how grateful he is for my friendship and for God's blessing of me in his life. Each time, I let him know that it is truly reciprocal—he is the other half of the miracle that God physically manifested in both our lives. I am genuinely grateful for his presence in my life and what it has done to deepen my relationship with Jesus and to set me free from the pain of my past trauma.

> *Trust in the Lord with all your heart and lean*
> *not on your own understanding; In all your ways*
> *acknowledge Him, and He shall direct your paths.*
> (Proverbs 3:5–6)

CHAPTER 9

—— ⌘ ——

Lessons Learned

I have learned so much on my more-than-forty-year journey. It is my hope that by sharing some of these lessons, I might help others who need to forgive and/or those who desire to establish a relationship with Jesus and deepen their faith in God.

Lesson 1: When I put God first in my life, anything is possible, even the impossible.

My life improved when I turned back to God; however, when I started to put God *first* in my life, it changed drastically. This is what led to the miracle that occurred in my life—my full healing and my ability to love the man I once hated. What does it mean to put God first? It means understanding that God is the most important Being in my life. It means understanding that without God, I am nothing, and with God, anything is possible in my life, even the impossible. I never imagined that I could reach full healing, and I certainly never envisioned becoming friends with the man who caused so much pain in my life and killed my friend. However, God makes things happen in our lives that we do not expect or that we cannot imagine.

For with God nothing is impossible. (Luke 1:37)

In order to prioritize anything or anyone in our lives, we must make time; therefore, I needed to start making time for God beyond just fulfilling my Sunday obligation of going to mass. In order to put God first, I needed to understand Him. The only way to understand God and what He expects of us is to establish a relationship with His Son Jesus Christ through prayer and reading The Word.

> *Your word is a lamp to my feet and a light to*
> *my path.* (Psalm 119:105)

Although I had a somewhat established habit of prayer, I learned that I needed to build in regular prayers of thanksgiving—thanking God for the many blessings, big and small, He had bestowed on me throughout my life. No matter what we have been through in our lives, there is always something that we should be grateful for—our relationships, our job, our financial situation, our friendships, one more day on earth, etc. God wants to hear that we recognize the gifts He has given to us. Through prayer, we can even thank God for things that have not happened yet in our lives. I have thanked Him many times for bringing this book to publication as I write it.

> *Praise the Lord! Praise God in his sanctuary;*
> *praise him for his mighty firmament! Praise him for*
> *his mighty deeds.* (Psalm 150: 1–2)

I also learned that I needed to look beyond my life by praying for others—people I know, as well as people I do not know. We all have friends, coworkers, and family members who are experiencing difficulties, and we can pray for God to strengthen them and support them through their trials. However, it is also important to pray for people we do not know—the poor, the homeless, nonbelievers, the unemployed, etc. When we do this, we are praying for humanity—that we may become a nation and world that cares about all its people, especially those in most need. This is so important, especially now with the rise in racism and violence in our country.

> *He pled the cause of the afflicted and needy;*
> *Then it was well. Is not that what it means to know*
> *Me?" Declares the Lord.* (Jeremiah 22:16)

God also wants us to ask Him to bring to fruition the desires we have in our heart. He wants to know our needs and wants. This was hard for me to do initially. It has always been easy for me to pray for others, but asking God for something to benefit me did not come easy. Who am I to ask God for something? Am I worthy? I have come to learn that I am—we all are. We are all almighty children of the Most High God! If God has put a dream in our heart, we need to ask Him to bring it to fulfillment.

> *Until now you have asked nothing in my*
> *name. Ask, and you will receive, that your joy may*
> *be full.* (John 16:24)

In addition to the importance of prayer, I learned that I need to know what is in the greatest book ever written—the Bible. When I attended the CRHP weekend and the Alpha course, I was embarrassed to even admit that the only time I read the Bible was when I was selecting scripture for my parents' funerals. I never saw either of my parents read the Bible as I was growing up. We had several Bibles in our house, but no one ever read them. In fact, I received my dad's Bible after he died, and it has been sitting on my bedside table since 2012. I never felt a need to read it, and anyway, how would I find time? After the CRHP weekend, I joined the planning team for the following year's retreat weekend. We met regularly the year leading up to the retreat, and during each meeting, we spent time reading and reflecting on a piece of scripture—I soon found myself hooked. A few months later, I enrolled in my first Bible study. As of the writing of this chapter, I am at the end of my third Bible study and look forward to our next one. Reading the Bible and talking about it with others proved to be a great way for me to get started with learning the Word.

Peter once told me that the word *Bible* is an acronym for *Basic Instruction Before Leaving Earth*. I always thought the Bible was scary and that I would not understand it. Certainly, there are scripture passages that are harder to understand than others, but what I have learned is that the Bible truly does have "basic instruction" for life, especially the New Testament books. While I am still a novice, I have learned so much about what the Lord expects of us and the promises (over six thousand!) He has made to us if we remain faithful. It has also been fascinating to learn of the history of humanity and to see the repeated mistakes God's people have made, even when they knew His expectations. There are so many parallels to current-day situations, especially the issues we are facing with the COVID-19 pandemic and the rise in racism and Black Lives Matter movement. The more things change, the more they stay the same! I have made many connections and have found great relevance to today's issues in the scriptures. Most importantly, through reading the Word, I have deepened my relationship with Jesus. How amazing is it that we can actually read the words Jesus spoke to His disciples and others of His time? This is truly a precious gift!

I also learned that God does not expect us to stop with just *reading* the Bible—He expects us to *do* what is in the Bible in order to become better people. In Mark 12:28–31, Jesus is asked, "Which commandment is the first of all?" Referred to as the Great Commandment, Jesus answered, "And you shall love the Lord your God with all your heart, and with all your soul, and with all your mind, and with all your strength. The second is this, you shall love your neighbor as yourself. There is no other commandment greater than these." Thus, if we keep God first in our lives, we might assume we are meeting the first part of the Great Commandment; however, we are not because the second part of the commandment is integral to the first. In order to love our God with all our heart, soul, mind, and strength, we have to love "our neighbor" because the way we treat others reflects directly on God. It is through our *actions* that we convey our love for God and for our neighbors. If we are good to others, we are good to God, but if we are hurtful, mean, dismissive to others, we are hurtful, mean, and dismissive to God. This is a tall order and one that I have had to work on with intentionality—it is a daily struggle. However, one of the things that I have learned is that when your heart becomes full of the love of God, it becomes much easier to "love your neighbor" and overlook the faults of others, resulting in kind and caring actions toward others.

As my heart became filled with God's love, my life changed because a heart full of God's love has little room for anger, bitterness, resentment, etc. I am less likely to react to stressful situations with anger—I use fewer foul words and "sign language" when driving and someone cuts me off, my stress and anxiety levels are lower, and my patience level is higher. This is not to say I never lose my cool or that my life is perfect—it is far from perfect, but God does not expect us to be perfect. We stumble and sometimes fall, but He is there to pick us up and put us back on the righteous path. The important thing is that we ask for forgiveness and for guidance and then work at being a better person each day.

As my relationship with God strengthened, I also learned that it is alright to express anger and frustration to Him. When something difficult happens, we need to let God know how we are feeling—tell Him about our anger, frustration, and pain. He wants to know.

> *Cast all your anxieties on Him, for He cares about you.* (1 Peter 5:7)

Then we need to ask for His help in getting through the pain or challenge we face. I wish I had understood this back in 1979. Perhaps if I did, I would not have turned my back on God and my faith.

Putting God first takes time, and time is of a premium in all of our lives, especially for those who have children, a demanding job, or any other situation that requires a lot of time. How in the world was I going to find time to pray and read the Bible regularly when my days were already full? What I learned is that I needed to reevaluate *how* I was spending my time. How much time was I spending on Facebook and other social media, playing games on my phone, and doing other activities on my computer? According to a MarketWatch article by

Quentin Fottrell on August 4, 2018, "In the first quarter of the year, U.S. adults spent three hours and 48 minutes a day on computers, tablets and smartphones." I would suspect that today, the amount of time is likely even higher for many of us. Think about some of the junk we are reading about/listening to in these almost four hours a day? If we just give up one-eighth of that time, we will have thirty minutes a day to pray and read a passage or two of scripture. I made the excuse for many years that I did not have time; I learned that I just needed to reevaluate *how* I was spending my time.

In his podcast, Pastor Rick Warren shares a strategy for making time with the Bible that some readers may find helpful. He calls it "His Word First Word, His Word Last Word." Pastor Rick suggests that we keep a Bible on our bedside table and leave it open. When we wake up, we start reading a passage on that page and read until we get to a point at which we make a personal connection and then take a few minutes to reflect on what we read. We then leave the Bible open to that page, and when we go to bed, we pick up reading where we left off in the morning and continue this process. There are also several daily devotions, both in print and electronic formats—*Our Daily Bread, Beside the Still Waters,* Joel and Victoria Osteen's *Today's Word,* Pastor Rick Warren's Daily Hope—that could be a good starting point. Additionally, there is also a phone app called *You Version* that allows the user to set up an individual Bible reading plan. For example, there is a plan for reading the Bible in a year, and the app will guide the user through the plan. Whatever strategy is used, I have found that establishing a routine that works for me is what will ensure that I continue to read the Word, and it becomes habit.

When I put God first in my life, He prepared me for the act of mercy I would put forth in July 2019. He pursued me for decades and put me exactly where I needed to be each time I moved so that He could subtly bring me back to my Catholic faith and closer to Him. Then a month or so prior to putting in my heart that I should write that letter, He led me to two faith groups. I have no doubt that this was to ensure that I had support for that difficult task. Everything was carefully orchestrated by God. That is what He does if we let Him and we put Him first in our lives.

Questions for reflection:

1. How would you describe your relationship with God?
2. Do you want to change your relationship in any way? If so, how?
3. What is the first step you can take to build in a regular time for prayer and/or reading the Bible?

Lesson 2: Being part of a faith community enhances my relationship with God

In addition to putting God first in my life, I learned the importance of being part of a faith community. Prior to 2018, I attended mass each week, and that was the extent of my life in the church. On the way home from mass, my partner and I might talk about the message in the homily, but other than that, I did not think about the content of the mass until I went back the following week.

When God led me to the Alpha and CRHP ministries, I was blessed with many wonderful new men and women in my life. Both of these ministries opened the door to other opportunities of fellowship, including Bible studies and prayer groups. Prior to this, we had been attending mass at that church for eighteen years and knew no one other than a couple of our neighbors that happened to attend. Now when I go to church, I am surrounded by friends.

In addition to worshipping together, a faith community can get us through the tough times. When life gets challenging, I have so many brothers and sisters praying their hearts out for me. I wish I been part of a faith community back in 1979. Receiving support from others who are filled with the love of God can make the unbearable more bearable. With my current faith community and my deep faith, I know that I can get through anything now.

Carry each other's burdens, and in this way,
you will fulfill the law of Christ. (Galatians 6:2)

Questions for reflection:

1. What opportunities does your church provide for fellowship?
2. Which of the opportunities provided are of most interest to you? Which are most conducive to your life schedule and circumstances?
3. What is one step you can take to connect with a faith community?

Lesson 3: Trauma affects not only the survivor(s), but also the survivor's family members and friends

It goes without saying that Laura's family members and friends were devastated by their loss. But we must also think about the loss experienced by the survivors' family members and friends. One might think, what loss did they experience? They still have their loved one. When there is trauma like this, all victims are changed, and their previous selves are gone—all are lost. After November 29, 1979, I was no longer the person who walked into McDonald's that day—that innocent, naïve, happy young woman was gone—wiped off the face of the earth. I was changed forever. Unlike Laura, I was still living. My body was still here, but nothing else of me was left. I could only see life through traumatized eyes and think with my traumatized brain.

It did not dawn on me until forty years later that my family and close friends also experienced loss that night. The "old me" was gone, and they had to figure out how to communicate and interact with a fragile, scared, and very sad young woman—that could not have been easy. If we had all understood this in 1979, perhaps we could have navigated the challenging situation in a more positive manner. It is my hope that other survivor victims and their families will benefit from my reflections.

My message to the family members of survivors of a traumatic experience is to simply listen. The most important thing for me after the trauma was to be able to talk about that night and express my feelings and the impact it was having on me. However, because of the reactions I received when I tried to talk, I withdrew inward. I wanted people to understand how devastated I was by the experience. I felt like my life was over and that I would never experience happiness again. I just needed to be able to talk and have people listen, rather than tell me all the reasons why I should not feel the way I was feeling or try to change the subject because it was too uncomfortable.

Listening to someone talk about a horrific experience is not comfortable, and in fact, it can be devastating for the person listening. Our tendency is to say things to diffuse or lighten the severity of the feelings or say clichés like "you shouldn't feel that way," "I know how you feel," or "you have to move on." However, the survivor needs to tell the grim details of the trauma, sometimes over and over, and they need someone to simply listen and affirm their feelings. Let the survivor know you can see they have been profoundly impacted and acknowledge how difficult it must be to experience the feelings they are experiencing—validate what they are communicating. Avoid judgmental or dismissive statements at all cost. Express your love and care for them and assure the survivor that you are there to listen any time they need to talk. Do not try to say something that you think will fix it—as hard as it is, you have to accept that you cannot fix it.

My message to survivors is to communicate what you need and be sure to share your feelings with people you trust. Understand that people may say things that are not helpful and sometimes things that you think are downright stupid—just let them know you need them to simply listen. As hard as it is, be patient and understand that your loved ones likely have good intentions, but sometimes they are just not sure how to help. I made the mistake of turning away from my family and friends—do not make that same mistake. We need our family and friends more than ever after a traumatic experience—we cannot go through a crisis alone and come out healthy.

Ecclesiastes 3:1, 7: *"For everything there is a season, and a time for every matter under heaven; a time to tear and a time to sew; a time to keep silence, and a time to speak."*

Questions for reflection:

1. If you are a survivor, are there people you have pushed away that you want back in your life? If so, what is your plan to communicate with them?
2. If you are a survivor, do you need to improve your communication with someone in your life? If so, what changes will you make?
3. When someone talks to you about a challenge/problem, do you listen and provide affirmation? What improvements do you need to make in your listening/affirmation skills?

Lesson 4: People make mistakes, some of which have excruciating consequences, but one moment in time should not define a person for the rest of his/her life.

We have all made mistakes in our lives. Fortunately, from most of these mistakes, we can "recover," leaving minimal long-term consequences. However, there are some mistakes that are made that have devastating and far reaching consequences. When adolescents and young adults make mistakes, there are additional factors to consider. Recent brain research shows that the frontal lobe of the brain, that part which affects reasoning, impulse, and judgment, does not fully develop until the midtwenties. "Young adults are more similar to adolescents than fully mature adults in important ways. They are more susceptible to peer pressure, less future-oriented and more volatile in emotionally charged settings" (*Washington Post*, October 4, 2015). As a result, adolescents and young adults do not think the way adults, with fully developed brains, think.

Most of us can probably recall "stupid" things we did in our adolescent or young adult years. I personally thank God that some of the things that I did as a young adult, such as driving under the influence, did not result in severe consequences. Furthermore, some of us can imagine a situation in which an adolescent or young adult that we know could find themselves in an environment in which guns and alcohol/drugs are present. Because most adolescents and young adults are not yet capable of reasoning the way adults are, they are not thinking of what could happen when guns are handled by someone under the influence.

In Peter's case, the situation was further confounded by the financially desperate state of mind in which he found himself. Peter and his sixteen-year-old girlfriend were not fully capable of understanding what could possibly go wrong—the devastation they could and did cause—as their plan to rob the McDonald's unfolded. Their still-developing minds were only thinking about the current financial need and how to get quick money.

While I was very pleased with the natural life sentence Peter received back in 1981, I now believe that such a sentence was excessive based on his age at the time of the crime. He was not mentally capable of understanding the consequences of his actions as he walked into McDonald's, high on drugs and alcohol, with a gun in his hand. I suspect that his race also played a role in the length of the sentence. These factors, combined with Peter's genuine and diligent effort to reform and develop into a true disciple of God, have convinced me that the natural life sentence was not justice in his case. My faith and deep understanding of God's mercy and forgiveness have also caused my change of heart. Peter made a mistake that had devastating consequences, but it was a mistake. God forgives him, and so must I if I am to be forgiven for my sins. He deserves a second chance to live outside of the prison walls as a changed man—a man of God who can benefit society through his ministry of others. I would want the same for my brother, uncle, or nephew if they made a mistake of this magnitude as an adolescent or young adult.

Questions for Reflection:

1. Is there something in your own life that you did when you were an adolescent/young adult for which you need to forgive yourself?
2. If there is something for which you need to forgive yourself, why have you not been able to forgive yourself? What will help you take steps to forgive yourself?

Lesson 5: Everything that happens in my life is part of God's plan for me—I might not initially understand, but I need to trust God.

God has a plan for each of our lives. We have a choice—to believe this and let God lead us or to take our lives into our own hands and try to find our way. I have taken both of these routes, and I found that letting God lead my life results in much better outcomes and less anxiety and stress. This has required me to trust—trust that God knows what should happen in my life and when it should happen in order to get me to the purpose He has for me. More specifically, it requires that I pray, listen, and then *accept* the outcome. As can be expected, it is really easy to trust God when things go the way we would like them to; however, it is much more difficult when the outcome is not what we expect or desire. And it is even more difficult when something happens in our life that we do not see coming.

I was blindsided in 1979, and it took me decades to understand why God put me there that night. At that time, I did not have any faith foundation on which to rely. As I moved forward, unbeknownst to me, God put me where I needed to be and put people in my life that would help me to build a spiritual foundation. He worked subtly in my life, through both good and bad experiences. One of these unexpected and bad experiences happened a few years ago, and I really struggled to understand why God would allow it to happen. I had been serving in a leadership role in my job for ten years and had been very successful in building solid programs and a strong departmental culture. One day I was told that I would no longer be in that leadership role and that the institution would be hiring a person outside of the institution to fill the role. Having been at the institution for eighteen years and in a leadership role for ten years, this initially came as a great shock and terrible disappointment—a personal attack. By that time in my life, I had fortunately reached the point where I was beginning to let God lead my life, and I quickly turned my mind to thinking "as hard as this is, God has a purpose for this unexpected turn in my life." I was certain that this was part of God's plan for me because as I sat and listened to the administrators telling me about their decision, I had an incredible calm about me that I have never experienced during challenging/stressful situations.

My typical response would have been tears, but it was as if God had taken over my body and I just sat there with a sense of peace and calm as I listened to them.

> Psalm 37:23–24: *"The steps of a man are established by the Lord, when he delights in his way; though he fall, he shall not be cast headlong, for the Lord upholds his hand."*

When challenges come our way, we can embrace them as part of God's plan, or we can respond with anger, sadness, or other negative emotions. Why were they treating me like this? I have been a devoted employee for almost twenty years. I could have wallowed in pity, looking for the sympathy of others and complaining about the way I was treated. Of course, I did some of that initially, but had I stayed in that mind-set for very long, my heart would have been so full of anger, sadness, and bitterness—I would have become a miserable person. As I prayed about what had happened, my heart was consoled, and I knew that there was a reason for what was happening in my life. I just needed to trust God.

> Proverbs 3:5: *"Trust in the LORD with all your heart, and do not lean on your own understanding."*

It did not take long for me to see God's reason for this change in my life—the gift of time. The result of being relieved of my leadership responsibilities was an increased amount of time to engage in activities outside of work. I no longer had to be on campus all day, every day and throughout the summer months. This was God setting the stage—providing me with the time to get involved in activities at my church and the time to attend daily mass on a regular basis. All of this was leading me to a deeper relationship with God. This deeper relationship with Him is what led to me write the letter to Peter and subsequently brought me to full forgiveness through the development of a beautiful friendship. Had I not experienced that incredible disappointment at work and made the choice to accept it as God's plan for me, my life would be very different today. What I thought was a horrible injustice ended up being a critical part of the path to my full healing, creating an overabundance of love in my heart.

Psalms 118:23: "*This is the Lord's doing; it is marvelous in our eyes.*"

Life is too short to spend it with anger, frustration, resentment, or bitterness in our hearts. I have learned to live life to the fullest, and the best way to do that is to trust that everything that happens in my life is part of God's plan. Does that mean that I think the injustice that was done to me was right? No, I do not, but I can rejoice for all the good that He has created in my life through that injustice, and I need to use the bad things that happen to *develop* my character and make me a better person, rather than let them *define* or *destroy* me.

Questions for Reflection:

1. Is there something disappointing that happened in your life that you can now see happened for a reason?
2. When something bad happens, how do you typically respond? What changes would you like to make the way you respond when something bad happens?

Lesson 6: Forgiveness is the way to full healing.

Forgiveness is a choice from a human perspective, but as a Christian, it is an expectation. God sent His only Son to earth to endure suffering and a horrible death so that our sins could be forgiven. The pain and agony that Jesus experienced for us is hard to even imagine. Oddly, my first understanding of the depth of His suffering occurred when I was on a family vacation as a young girl. One of the best vacations on which my parents took me and my younger brother was to the Badlands. We visited many tourist attractions on that trip, but the one that still remains vivid and special in my memory is seeing the passion play enacted in an outdoor theatre. As a ten-year-old at the time, I always thought it was amazing that this was my most treasured memory, but now it makes clear sense. Of course, I did not have the full understanding of what Jesus did for us at that age, but the fact that I was so impacted by that reenactment speaks volumes to the role that this early experience played in my spiritual journey.

For years, I lived with hatred in my heart. It caused me to be racist, angry, sad, and depressed. As one can imagine, life was not enjoyable—in fact, it was miserable. Once I made the choice to forgive Peter many years ago, my life was definitely more joyful, but there was still something "nagging" at me, making it difficult to let go of the trauma fully. Not all victims will have the chance to tell the person who wronged them that they are forgiven; however, this is when my life truly became filled with joy. When I wrote the letter, I was doing it for Peter—so that he knew someone from that night forgave him. What I did not expect is the impact that it would have on me, bringing me to full healing from the trauma of that night. An important part of my full healing was hearing from Peter that he was truly remorseful, which was very clear from the moment we met in the prison on October 5, 2019, and continues to be clear as I talk with him daily.

Forgiveness set me free from the negative emotions that had built up in my heart and brought me closer to God. The heavy burden that had been constraining me was lifted and no longer controls my life. My heart is full of love and joy, rather than hate and rage.

Questions for Reflection:

1. Is there someone in your life that you need to forgive? If so, what steps might you take?
2. If you need to forgive someone, but have not been able to, what is getting in the way? Is there anything you can do to work through whatever is stopping you? Are there people/resources who could help you work through the issues?

Lesson 7: We are a continual work of progress in the hands of God.

In a podcast I recently listened to, Joel Osteen made a comparison between how a potter creates a work on the potter's wheel and how God develops us. The potter starts with a lump of clay and uses his/her hands to shape the clay into the desired piece of work, finishing the piece by adding color and an appealing finish. The potter begins with a simple, plain piece of clay and creates a beautiful masterpiece. Likewise, God begins with a simple, plain human being and creates a beautiful masterpiece, each one of us uniquely constructed. As I reflected further on this analogy, I began thinking about one key factor that is unique to humans in this comparison. The clay is pliable, changing shape as the wheel spins, and the potter uses his/her hands to create the desired form. For the most part, there is not resistance, and the potter is able to achieve the shape and design that s/he envisions for each unique piece. God has a vision for each of us; however, we must also be pliable and allow Him to do the work in our lives, leading to His perfect masterpiece of each of us.

The actions that I discussed in lesson 1 played a huge role in allowing God to fully develop me. I found that my prayer life, time reading the Bible, and the fellowship with other parishioners, all enhanced my spiritual development. One key to this has been my openness—my willingness to consider opportunities that God has placed before me to deepen my faith and my willingness to engage in these opportunities when possible. For example, I was invited to join a group of men and women who pray the Rosary and the Chaplet of Divine Mercy each night on Zoom. Not all members of the group are present every night, allowing people to join when it works in their schedule. As I considered this opportunity, I thought about what I would normally be doing during that hour in the evening—checking e-mail and doing other things on my computer. It did not take me long to figure out that being involved in prayer for an hour is a much more productive use of my time, so I joined the group. In the past, I probably would have declined the offer, thinking that it was something I did not have time to do. This prayer session has become one of the highlights of my day—we pray for each other, people in our lives that need prayer, people from our parish who have requested prayer, groups of people in society that are in most need of prayer, and for the variety of issues that plague our nation.

The other key is obedience. If we let God lead us, we must do what He asks us to do, even if we do not understand and/or are uncomfortable with what He puts before us. When God put in my heart to let Peter know that I forgave him, there were several moments in the process where I asked "you want me to do what?" It took me several months to send the letter. I am not sure why it took so long; however, had I ignored God's request, my life would be very different right now.

> *Oh, that you had heeded my Commandments!*
> *Then your peace would have been like a river, and*
> *your righteousness like the waves of the sea.* (Isaiah
> 48:18)

In order to become the masterpiece that God envisions for each of us, we must have full faith in Him and His path for our lives. This means we must trust Him in the good times and when life gets unbearably painful. Trust that He never leaves us, and we can always go to Him no matter how challenging life gets. Trust in the path that He has paved for each of us. At the beginning of my journey, I never thought it would be possible to reach full forgiveness and have peace in my heart. It took forty years and a lot of work, but He finally brought me home to Him, and the result was a true miracle.

> *For with God nothing will be impossible.*
> (Luke 1:37)

PRAYER TO THE READERS

D ear heavenly Father, I lift up in prayer and thank You for all who are reading this story of the miracle You manifested in mine and Peter's lives. I pray that each person is filled with a deeper understanding of Your will and the way You work in each of our lives for our good. Father God, please manifest Your healing virtue in a miraculous way in anyone who is in need of healing and please help to mend the hearts of those who need to forgive or be forgiven. Lord, please fill each person with Your love so that there is no room for hatred, bitterness, or anger in our hearts. You have started a work in us and I pray that You will direct the steps of each person reading this story to the purpose You have for them and shower each with Your abundant love, grace, mercy, and peace this day and every day. Father God, please bless and keep each person and may Your face shine upon us and may You lift up Your countenance upon us and give us peace. I pray all of this in the name of Your precious Son, Jesus Christ. Amen.

APPENDIX A

Maureen's First Letter to Peter

July 16, 2019

Peter,

I am one of the six women who were in the McDonald's in Oak Forest November 29, 1979 when you robbed the store and killed my friend, Laura. I am writing to tell you that I forgive you. I hope this means something to you, as I am not writing this for me--this is not part of therapy, which is what one could think. Rather, I am writing this for you, Peter. I forgave you many years ago but recently, a thought popped into my mind that I should tell you. I believe that was God/Jesus letting me know that you deserve to know that at least one of us forgives you.

It has been a forty-year journey for me with emotions ranging from complete hatred of you to my current feelings of empathy for you. My journey has been very difficult but, with the help of God, I now can see beyond my own experience and needs to how difficult this has had to be on you. As a nineteen-year-old young man, I now know you made a mistake—a big mistake—one that has resulted in you living your life in the prison system, which I know cannot be easy. I am sorry for that—I truly am.

I don't know what life has been like for you all these years after the crime you committed—maybe you don't even ever think about that night or us. But if there are some remnants of memories and any guilt, I pray that hearing from at least one of us that you are forgiven will bring you peace, Peter. I also pray that you have asked God for forgiveness, as he is merciful and forgives all who ask, no matter what the sin.

You may not care at this point about hearing from any of us, but I wanted to write in case it is important for you to hear this—I forgive you, Peter. I know some people find God/Jesus in prison—I pray you are one of those people. If not, there is still time. God can bring you peace and mercy if you ask for guidance and forgiveness, Peter. *"If we confess our sins, He is faithful and just to forgive us our sins and to cleanse us from all unrighteousness."* 1 John 1:9.

I am not what some people would call a "Jesus freak" or some-one trying to convert you to a religion. I'm an ordinary person, who happens to be Christian (Catholic) and as I pray each day, I try to listen to what God is telling me to guide me. Over the forty years that I have dealt with the pain of that night, He has guided me and helped me to deal with my pain and anguish as a survivor. And He led me to writing this letter to let you know that I forgive you. I pray that it means something to you, but I also know that it may not, and I'm ok with that. But if it does mean something to you, God's work has been done.

I have included a stamped envelope with this letter (addressed to me at my church's address) in case you want to respond to me. But I certainly don't expect that if you choose not to. May God's Grace and Mercy bring peace and comfort to you the rest of your life on earth, Peter. *"The Lord is gracious and full of compassion, slow to anger and great in mercy. The Lord is good to all, and His tender mercies are over all His works."* Psalm 145:8-9. Ask for his forgiveness and you will be forgiven, and He will welcome you into his kingdom when your time on earth is done if you believe in Him. Until then, may God bless and keep you in the palm of his hand, Peter.

Peace be with you,

~Maureen

APPENDIX B

Peter's First Letter to Maureen

7-28-19.

Maureen,

I truly thank you for taking time to write me a heart felt letter letting me know that you forgave me for the crimes I committed 40 years ago. I am very sorry for all the pain, hurt, heartache, mental and emotional anguish I caused the ████████ family love ones, friends and co-workers who were very near and dear to Laura ████████.

Your letter was the answer to our prayers. It came from the heart and touch our hearts and caused us to weep, giving thanks and praises to God. Most definitely an act of God's spirit working in you both to will and to do of His good pleasures. Maureen it's no doubt God's work has been done! Thank you so very much for forgiven me. And I am very sorry for everything that you had to go through in the last 40 years over the loss of your dear friend and co-worker Laura ████████.

Thank you for allowing God to help you to persevere through your 40 year journey of emotional rage and hatred of me to your current feelings of empathy for me. To God be the glory for the great and wonderful things He has done in you and through you by all means.

Maureen, I did repent and I confessed my sins many days and nights after my arrest. I stayed on my knees in jail cells and prison cells talking to God. He heard my cry and delivered me from a life of destruction. He forgave me of my sins and cleansed me from all unrighteousness. God is near to those who have broken heart and saves such as have a contrite spirit (Psalm 34:18).

89

My uncle was my Pastor, and my mother and I went to church every Sunday and Prayer Meeting on Wednesday. I went astray and into a backslidden state of a world of sin and in bondage to drugs and alcohol. I drop out of college, I was without a cause, lost, no sense of direction and without hope. My girlfriend was pregnant Months from given birth to a baby.

Now that I am a born again believer, I can testify of the goodness of God that leads us to Repentance. I am a living testimony and a living witness of God love, mercy and Grace. God has been the source of my strength and the strength of my life, helping me to undergo the death of my Beloved Mother and my Beloved Son who has been welcome in His Kingdom along with Laura ▋. This has been a very difficult 40 year journey something I would not have been able to do this on my own. I truly thank God for the help He provided and the special people He put in my life to enable me to persevere and endure the hardship from the things I encountered throughout the years of my incarceration. His Grace has been sufficient, and His strength has been made perfect in my weakness.

I empathize with the people that I hurt and caused Heartache and Pain. I have experience many sleepless Night and often cried myself to sleep. To this day I still grieve over the death of Laura ▋ and continue to pray for Her Family, love ones and friends and co workers.

Maureen, your letter of forgiveness, empathy, and genuine concern was well received with thanksgiving and Praise. I pray that God will continue to use you to bring to pass His purpose, Plan and will in the lives of the people you know and meet. I pray that God will continue to bless you and keep you and be gracious to you as His face shine with

Pleasure upon you as you walk in the light of
His Countenance, May He give you Peace, Tranquility
of heart with joy unspeakable and life Continually
in Jesus name. Maureen you have sown many tears
you shall reap in Joy (Psalm 126:5).

I have accepted Full responsibility for the
regrettable actions I took on November 29, 1979
as a drunken 19 year old I.V. drug user, drug addict
who was looking for quick Cash. While my heartache
and remorse over the unintended loss of the life
of Laura ██████████ has grown through the years So has
my character, integrity, intellect, kindness, spirituality,
and Commensurate Commitment to make a positive
difference in Someone's life. I desperately want to
use my experience to benefit Schools, organizations,
communities, neighborhoods, associations, institutions,
agencies and programs where the prevention of teen
Criminal pursuit is a priority.

I am well aware of the recent research on the
development of the Frontal lobe of the brain. That
part of the brain Controls judgement and decision
making. We now Know that this significant Frontal
lobe development is not Complete until humans are
in their mid 20's. I am not making excuses for my
terrible crime. However, I must emphasize that
the immature, drug addicted 19 year old kid who
Committed that tragic Crime no longer exists.
As a mature, nurturing and Committed adult,
Man of Faith I will Continue to seek the Lord in

prayer that one day I be granted release so that I can benefit Society and use the lessons of my past to give so many others a brighter future.

With my tremendous insight on how caring communities can be more responsive in reaching out to hopeless youth, I can help so many school officials, civic, social, religious and business leaders find more creative ways to develop character, enhance academic achievement and improve the school performance of underachieving "hopeless" youth. My desire to make such a positive difference in other lives is not only admirable but insatiable. I am both a living example of the consequences of lost hope in impressionable school age youth, and a model example of what restored hope can do to rehabilitate a convicted felon.

Many years ago, my beloved sister, my minister of the gospel and spiritual mentor and counsel, who has been there for me every step in this journey, copyrighted the phrase, "Merchants of Hope" to describe those person who are committed to enriching other lives. Although it was "hopelessness and despair" that guided me on the night of November 29, 1979, I have become an inspirational "Merchant of Hope" to many of the staff, officers and many inmates I have met and mentored during my 40 years of incarceration. I am a caring, considerate, kind, compassionate, charismatic, committed and competent. Others outside of the prison walls should be allowed to benefit from my craving for knowledge and the many exemplary qualities that have made me a "Model Prisoner." I believe that God has blessed me to be a remarkable example of the efforts of the Illinois Department of Corrections to "rehabilitate and prevent recidivism." Me

longer a "Threat to Society" I am laudable and news
worthy example of how a lost teen can be transformed
into a life enriching adult. I am a child of God by all
means, a God fearing man pursuing righteousness, godliness,
Faith, love, Patience, gentleness, & devoted man of
Prayer, Something that I know God has blessed me
teach and share with others along with Forgiveness.

I received your letter 7-22-17. I pray that God
will continue to help us to overcome our struggles, help
us to undergo our daily demand's and our routines in
Jesus name.

Maureen, it is well with my soul and I am in a Peaceful
state of mind. May you continue to be used by God For
His Glory, Honor, and Praise. Your labor is not in vain.

Enclosed is a few things I accomplished. Something
I thought would be nice to share with you.

I pray your church will continue to do the will of
God by all means. I pray the People of the Church will
succeed in all their endeavors, that their prayer be
answered, dreams come true, I pray God will make
their ways prosperous and they be blessed with good
success in Jesus name. God Bless you
                    Our Lady of Mercy

                    Sincerely,
                    Brother Peter Guy Logan

APPENDIX C

Maureen's Second Letter to Peter

August 9, 2019

Dear Peter,

When I received an email from the church secretary that I had a letter to pick up, my heart sank and I was filled with both nervousness and excitement, as I wasn't sure I would hear back from you. When I went to pick it up at the office and saw that the envelope was big and that it was obviously filled with more than just a letter, I was overwhelmed. I took it into the church and as I saw all the documentation of what you have done to better yourself and to give praise to Our Lord and Savior, I felt a huge sense of relief, knowing that you found God and have been doing so much to show your devotion to His Son by reading The Word and teaching others about the tremendous love of Our Father and His Son. Then I read your letter and just wept—with joy and with sadness. Joy that my letter touched your heart and was a sign of God's true love, because it truly was—God let me know that it was important for me to tell you that I forgave you. I also wept with sadness that you have had to live all of these years incarcerated.

I am so happy you have asked for God's forgiveness and He has given you such strength to endure these 40 years in the prison system and more importantly, the strength to help others in the prison system to see hope and have faith in the Greatness of Our Heavenly Father! The excerpt from the letter from Mike Frizzell and the other documents that show your participation in biblical studies/programs, as well as a degree in Theology studies are truly a testament to the work you have done to come closer to Jesus, study His Word and to help others in the prison system do the same. And your expressed desire to help schools, communities, neighborhoods, etc. to help "hopeless youth" is no doubt sincere. Praise God for his work through you, Peter!! You had a choice in how you handled your life in prison, and you chose GOD.

As you wrote about the research related to the development of the brain and the delay in its full development until the mid-20s, I fully understand that as I am a Professor of Education who prepares future teachers. I think that is why this has all come full circle for me as God has guided me in my journey and He taught me to understand that I needed to forgive you and have empathy for you. Now this is further impacted by the fact that I just learned last week that the son of a close family friend is facing felony gun possession charges and has a court date next week. I ask that you please pray that he will find his way. As I think about your circumstances, he could easily go down that road of making a big mistake, as he is drinking and getting high with a gun in his possession. And he could end up in prison, as you did. God has brought these two worlds colliding for me this week—a forty-year journey of healing and working on forgiveness and now a dear family friend is engaging in the same dangerous behavior you were engaging in when you were his age. That is God's work at hand bringing this all together. I pray that your story can help him, as I'm not sure what will get through to him. I will tell him about your story with the hopes that he will understand the grave consequences that could occur, even though I know his brain is not capable of truly understanding. If there is anything you can write to him to help him understand, please include it if you write back to me. And please pray for him, Peter.

I am so happy that you have had your sister to guide you all these years. I love her phrase "Merchant of Hope" and I am so happy you are serving in that role for those who you have encountered during your 40 years of incarceration. I am so sorry that you lost your son and your mother. But praise be to God that you have had support and love of many to help you all of these years.

I have two requests for you. May I share your letter with two of the other women that I have contact with who were there that night? I don't know where any of them are with their journey to healing and if they would want to read it, but I would like to offer that to them if you give me permission. Second, I would like to visit with you in person, Peter. Only, of course, if you believe this would help you and if you would like to meet. I honestly will not be offended if you do not, so please be honest. Again, this is not at all part of the healing process for me—God has truly guided me to reach out to you and help you in any way that I can. Think about it and let me know. If it's not good now for you, that doesn't mean it can't happen ever. If you would like a visit, please let me know the process for setting that up.

I am grateful that God has brought us together, Peter. He has a purpose for everything, and I am sure that this is only the beginning of his purpose for both of us. I am so happy you are at peace and that God is using you for His Glory, Honor and Praise. Continue to do His Work, Peter as you will be rewarded daily with His Grace and Mercy and with Life Everlasting when your time on this earth ends.

God Bless you, my brother in Christ,

Maureen

APPENDIX D

Peter's Second Letter to Maureen

8.18.19

(1)

Greetings, My Beloved Sister in Christ, Maureen

I pray this letter Find you at your best
in health, spirit and in a peaceful state of
mind. As of myself, all is truly well and
peaceful at this stage in my life. I am exceedingly
glad with the fullness of Joy because of you
Once again was I touch by your letter and
the love of God that exude from your heart.
My Beloved Sister in Christ, you are most definitely
Spirit Filled and has been blessed with the
Spirit of discernment, who can share the letters
I wrote you with anyone your heart desire
I know that you are truly lead and guided by
the Spirit of God and you have my best interest
at heart. Also I would love to behold the
Physical Manifestation of a blessing and the
Miracle working of Power of God with you on
a visit. That May be the best of the First day
of His Purpose in our lives. I have enclosed a
visiting list for you to complete and send back
to me so I can mail it in to get approved
The address you have on your Driver's license
need to be on the visiting list. Week days 4 hour
visits and weekend 2 hour you must be signed
in before 2:30pm the visiting open at 8:30am

97

2) I may receive 4 or 5 visit in a year and sometime not that many. Just so you can have the right intro. It will best for you to call here 309.343-4212 They do have Vendor Machine so you may want to purchase a Card and put some money on it if you are able. I need to let you know, thanks for taking time out to spend with me, that's joy unspeakable and God at work in our lives, I'm very excited. I will fast a day before you come visit me. I believe in truth and honesty so you never need to second guess me dealing in falsehood, I despise liars and it's a complete turn off. Also the word of God says all liars shall have their part in the lake which burns with fire and brimstone.

There's 4 people who I would like for you to call. Crystal, who is my beloved sister who would ~~like to speak with you~~ and most likely pray. Linda, who would like to meet you in person and see if she help out with ~~_____~~ My Attorney Ernesto Borges. would like to know the County ~~_____~~ was change in, Last but not Least, James Gibson who was Exonerated April 26, 2019 after spending 29 years in Prison for something he wrongful convicted of, he would like to share with you the major rule God Blessed me to have in his life while incarcerated. And thank you once again for doing this us and to the Glory of God.

8.18-19

Let us go boldly to the throne of Grace that we may obtain Mercy and Find grace to help in time of need. My Beloved Sister let us worship our Heavenly Father, in the beauty of His Holiness, Blessed are you, Our Father Forever and ever. Yours, O Lord is the greatness the power and the glory the victory and the Majesty For all that is in heaven and in earth is yours For yours is the Kingdom and you are exalted as Head over all Both riches and honor come From you and you reign over all In your Hand is power and Might and your Hand it is to make great And to give strength to all. We thank you and Praise Your glorious Name and all those Attributes that your Name denotes we worship you For who You are and everything that you are Making possible in our lives and others. you are amazing, and Wonderful, you are our bridge over trouble Water, and your Name is a strong tower where the righteous run and are Safe, We ask that you continue to keep us Protected From all hurt, harm and danger seen as well as unseen And Continue to strengthen us in time of weakness though we walk in the Midst of trouble you will Revive us and stretch out your Hand

against the wrath of our enemies your
right Hand will save us and you will perfect
that which concern us by all Means, let it
be unto us that you lead us and guide and
enable us to be everything that you purpose us
to be one to another, We ask that you have your
Way in our lives that we will be use by you
to impact other and Make a diffences in
their lives For your Glory, Honor and Praise
We are grateful unto you For bringing us
together For such time and season as this and
Know that all things will work together For
our good because of the love we have For you
and know that we have been call according to
your purpose, We commend ▬▬▬ unto you
to the word of your grace that is possible in
building him up and given him a purpose to serve
in this life, enable him to make himself known to
you that he may Find peace and good will come
to him as he read your word and hide it in his
heart and walk upright before, We ask that he
be save and healed From distress and delivered
From destruction, do what only you able to transform
his life by all means, you have proved yourself be
A very present helper in time of trouble, we ask
all these things in Jesus Name (So be it)

(4) I enjoyed praying with you And being there
for Me. It's no doubt the best is yet to Come
and our Heavenly Father will Continue to uphold our
steps in His path as we travel together down
this Christian journey and the walks in life.
No good thing will He with held from those who
walk upright before Him, let stay in right standing
with our Heavenly Father and acknowledge Him in
all our ways and let direct our path.
If you feel the need to hear Me by Phone, please
don't hesitate to ask Me to Call. Thank You for being
the person that you and a wonder in My life. Have a
blessed Day in an amazing Way.   Your Brother in Christ
                                                    Peter

ABOUT THE AUTHOR

Beginning her career as an elementary special education teacher and then as an educational consultant, Maureen Kincaid has been in the field of education for over 35 years, dedicating her life to improving the quality of education offered to elementary-aged children, with a focus on equity issues. After receiving her Doctor of Education (Ed. D.) degree, Maureen began teaching at the college level, preparing future teachers and is currently a Professor of Education at North Central College in Naperville, Illinois.

As a cradle Catholic, Maureen initially turned her back on the church and God when tragedy crushed her life in 1979. After many years of struggling with the effects of the trauma, she eventually made her way back to the Catholic Church. For decades, she had a desire to write a book about her experience as a survivor in order to help others deal with the effects of post-traumatic stress syndrome (PTSD). It was not until 2018, when she experienced a deepening of faith, that she learned that there was another piece of the story that needed to be lived before the book could be written. God led her to the man who caused so much pain and trauma and out of this encounter came an outpouring of mercy, love, and compassion, that can only be created by our Heavenly Father. This spiritual renewal created a desire in Maureen's heart to tell her story, and in so doing, to share the Word of God and the miraculous ways He changes lives if we turn to Him.

CPSIA information can be obtained
at www.ICGtesting.com
Printed in the USA
LVHW030204240421
685422LV00005B/312